## Memory's Mist

In *Memory's Mist*, Jackie K. Cooper has written a thoughtful, poignant and gently humorous portrait of family, faith, and small town life in the South. Intimate, funny, sad, and honest, Cooper is an astute observer and a genial commentator. Deftly executed and compellingly readable, *Memory's Mist* transcends the memoir genre and offers a deeper and more substantive view of contemporary American society. Find a comfortable chair and enjoy Cooper's unique voice. Highly recommended.

—Sheldon Siegel,
*New York Times* best selling
author of *Perfect Alibi*.

From the simple pleasures of road trips and bear hugs to sage musings about friendship, social media, worshipping one's Maker and the evolution of family roles, one is both charmed and enlightened by the profound truths that surface in Jackie K. Cooper's beautiful new memoir, *Memory's Mist*. An ideal blend of humor, honesty and insights amid everyday observations, this book deserves to be cherished by a wide readership.

—Beth Webb Hart,
best-selling author of
*Moon Over Edisto* and *Love, Charleston*

*Memory's Mist* is comfort food for the reader's soul. Jackie's honest reflections of past and present will have you searching your own life for the joy found in simple things.

—Nicole Seitz, author of
*The Spirit of Sweetgrass* and *The Inheritance of Beauty*

*Endowed by*
TOM WATSON BROWN
*and*
THE WATSON-BROWN FOUNDATION, INC.

*Memory's Mist*

The View from the Journey

Jackie K. Cooper

MERCER UNIVERSITY
MACON, GEORGIA

MUP/ P476

© 2013 Mercer University Press
1400 Coleman Avenue
Macon, Georgia 31207
All rights reserved

First Edition

Books published by Mercer University Press are printed on acid-free paper that meets the requirements of the American National Standard for Information Sciences—Permanence of Paper for Printed Library Materials.

Mercer University Press is a member of Green Press Initiative (greenpressinitiative.org), a nonprofit organization working to help publishers and printers increase their use of recycled paper and decrease their use of fiber derived from endangered forests. This book is printed on recycled paper.

ISBN      978-0-88146-464-1

Cataloging-in-Publication Data is available from the Library of Congress

*For Virginia "Ginnie" Kelly Cooper,*

*the last grandchild and the one with the gleam in her eyes*

## Contents

| | |
|---|---|
| Acknowledgments | xi |
| Foreword by Dale Cramer | xii |
| | |
| Prologue | 1 |
| Reflections from Route 2006 | 3 |
|     Look at Your Children and See Immortality | 5 |
|     Give Me a Car and Watch Me Drive | 7 |
|     Dance, Everyone, Dance | 9 |
|     The Roles Have Changed | 11 |
|     Dog Gone | 13 |
|     Every Face a Memory | 15 |
|     Happiness Is Just | 17 |
|     Some Promises Can't Be Kept | 19 |
|     The Best Book Festival Ever | 21 |
|     Just in Case | 23 |
|     Fear Itself | 25 |
|     Goodbye Was Long Ago | 27 |
|     Truth Be Told | 29 |
|     What's Faith Got to Do With It? | 31 |
|     Living in a Black and White World | 33 |
|     On the Radio | 35 |
|     When I Grow Up | 37 |
|     One Upmanship | 39 |
|     I Never Sang for My Father | 41 |
|     Out of the Mouths of Babes | 43 |
|     Old Fashioned | 45 |
|     Life Is a Vacation | 47 |
|     In Praise of Red-Headed Girls | 49 |
|     God Bless America | 51 |
|     Stop and Smell the Roses | 53 |

| | |
|---|---|
| When Is a Vacation Not a Vacation? | 55 |
| True Caring Makes for Good Care | 57 |
| Cell-O | 59 |
| Preparing for the Future | 61 |
| The Critic as Actor | 63 |
| Letters from Holland Street | 66 |
| Expectation vs. Anticipation | 68 |
| One Day at a Time | 70 |
| Biloxi—Blue but Not Defeated | 72 |
| Lonesome Town | 74 |
| Get Rid of the Blues with Jeans | 76 |
| Safe Alone | 78 |
| Give Me the Simple Life | 80 |
| Sweet Charity | 82 |
| Giving Thanks | 84 |
| My New Best Friend | 86 |
| Long Lasting Love | 88 |
| R-E-S-P-E-C-T | 90 |
| Christmas | 92 |
| It's Over | 94 |
| | |
| Reflections from Route 2007 | 97 |
| I've Found My Face | 99 |
| Talk Is Cheap | 101 |
| Foolish Fears | 103 |
| Idol Chatter | 105 |
| My Country 'Tis of Thee | 107 |
| Voices from the Past | 109 |
| A Trip to ABAC | 111 |
| Book People Are Special People | 113 |
| Durham | 116 |
| Missing Persons | 118 |
| What Is Celebrity? | 120 |
| Bless the Beasts and the Children | 122 |

| | |
|---|---|
| Making a Mountain out of a Big Hill | 124 |
| The Joy of Living | 126 |
| Someone to Watch Over Me | 128 |
| Online Dancing | 130 |
| Simply Southern | 132 |
| Hello Outdoors | 134 |
| A Gift from God | 136 |
| Like a Hole in the Head | 138 |
| A Trip to Memory | 140 |
| The Greatest Generation | 142 |
| A Week at the Beach | 144 |
| The Time Is Right, I Mean Ripe | 146 |
| You Are What You Car | 148 |
| My Mother the Car | 150 |
| The Great Outdoors | 152 |
| The Circle of Life | 154 |
| He's Flying the Plane | 156 |
| Now Is the Time | 158 |
| Who Killed the Cat? | 160 |
| An Angry Young Man | 162 |
| What Happened to Privacy? | 164 |
| All's Well That Ends Well | 166 |
| A Happy Birthday | 168 |
| The Accidental Author | 170 |
| Grieve Well, Heal Well | 173 |
| You Gotta, Gotta Have Friends | 175 |
| Fathers and Sons | 177 |
| It's Dangerous to Be Sick | 179 |
| Nature or Nurture | 181 |
| Dumpster Dating | 183 |
| One Door Shutting | 185 |
| Off to the Beach | 187 |
| And Then There Were Three | 189 |

| | |
|---|---|
| Travels with Jackie | 191 |
| My Uncle Frank | 193 |
| The Night after Christmas | 196 |

Reflections from Route 2008     199

| | |
|---|---|
| Be Aggressive | 201 |
| The More We Get Together | 203 |
| See Ya, St. John | 205 |
| Is the Building the Church? | 207 |
| You've Got to Have Sleep | 209 |
| What Are You Doing the Rest of Your Life? | 211 |
| My Buddy | 213 |
| The Art of Isolation Via E-Mails | 215 |
| Dream Big | 217 |
| A Reviewer's Life | 219 |
| Where Is the Cavalry? | 221 |
| Rumors of My Death | 223 |
| Talent Scouts | 225 |
| Father of a Preacherman | 227 |
| Like Father, Like Son etc.... | 229 |
| Shout to the Lord | 231 |
| A Weekend in the Country | 233 |
| Can You Hear Me Now? | 235 |
| Just Lock Me in the Car Again | 237 |
| Exercise Will Kill You | 239 |
| Try a Little Harder, Be a Little Better | 241 |
| The Way We Read | 243 |
| Walking Tall | 245 |
| The Write Stuff | 247 |
| Beat the Clock | 249 |
| Lonely Hearts | 251 |
| The Security of Sameness | 253 |
| The Dahlonega Literary Festival | 255 |
| My Friend Karen | 257 |

| | |
|---|---|
| Carry Me Back | 259 |
| About Facebook | 261 |
| Tomorrow | 263 |
| Highs and Lows | 265 |
| Magic Moments | 267 |
| Is That a Backlash I Hear? | 269 |
| What Happened to the Sting? | 271 |
| Nobody's Perfect | 273 |
| The Memory Keeper | 275 |
| The Georgia and Jackie Show | 277 |
| Guilt by Association | 279 |
| Is Honesty the Best Policy? | 281 |
| Love What's There | 283 |
| A Very Thankful Day | 285 |
| Season of Hope | 287 |
| Car Faith | 289 |
| Quiet Desperation | 291 |
| Yes, Santa Claus, There Is a Virginia | 293 |
| The Ballad of Bambo | 295 |
| Epilogue | 298 |

## *Acknowledgments*

First and foremost I want to thank Marc Jolley and all of his staff at Mercer University Press. A friendlier, more hardworking bunch of people you could not imagine. I love you all, but Marsha I have to admit I love you the best.

Also all of my writing friends. By example you lead me on my writing journey. You all know who you are and you know how much I cherish your friendships. Thank you from the bottom of my heart.

To my family: JJ and Angela, Sean and Paula, Genna and Walker, Natalie and Ginnie. No man could be more blessed. You all are my inspirations, my anchors in a stormy sea. My heart is brimful.

Finally to my wife Terry and my mother Virginia. My mother told me I was special and my wife makes me believe it.

## *Foreword*

Jackie Cooper is an unusual man.

Born and raised in Clinton, South Carolina (pronounced "Clinnon," for those of us who aren't from around there), Jackie's childhood was the Southern small-town version of ideal. But like many of us, once he got away from home he made some errant choices and his life took a grievous turn: he went to law school and became a lawyer. Later on he became an entertainment critic, reviewing books, plays, and movies in print and on television. Most of us would find it extremely difficult to overcome such tragic life choices, so I think it's a testament to Jackie's character and courage that he managed to pull it off. Somehow, in spite of being both a lawyer and a critic, Jackie Cooper is the happiest man I know— a fact that shatters some of my most cherished presuppositions.

I met him years ago at a book fair, and we became instant friends. It was a long time before it dawned on me that everybody who meets Jackie feels the same way. He and I have done a lot of events together since then— signings, author panels, interviews— and I always enjoy spending time with him. A big man with a big smile, Jackie's undiluted joie de vivre draws people like a magnet, and he's always glad to see them.

Here's the thing: there's no guile in him. That joy is genuine. At first blush, he appears to be a walking oxymoron—a lawyer who knows right from wrong, a critic with humility and compassion—and this puzzled me for years, until I finally figured out his secrets. There are two, and they work together.

First, at every major turning point in his life, Jackie has consistently chosen for love rather than money. He turned down a high-paying position in favor of a low-profile job in labor law because he knew it would give him more time with his family. In his spare time, he built a career as an entertainment critic simply because it's what he loves doing, and then spent a few years in California interviewing practically everybody in Hollywood. Many of his interviews are preserved today on YouTube, and it's well worth your time to look them up because the videos give you an idea of the man, and the voice, behind his stories. To date, Jackie has published six excellent collections of memoirs. His writing is warm and human and accessible, sort of a Southern Robert Fulghum. Even the stories from his later years take us back to a simpler time, a less complicated understanding of life and love and, yes, honor.

Jackie's other secret is equally simple, though less obvious: gratitude. He's unabashedly grateful for his life—his wife and sons, his friends, his work—and it shows up in his stories. He writes with humor, and without condescension; the foibles and failings in his memoirs are most often his own. Here you'll find none of the cynicism rampant in today's media, but gentle remembrances of a life well lived.

Love and gratitude. A pretty simple recipe, really, and it works. In a time of mass confusion and desperation, Jackie Cooper's memoirs are sketches of the sights and sounds along the path to joy.

Dale Cramer<br>
Award-winning author of<br>
*Bad Ground* and *Levi's Will*

## *Prologue*

As I have traveled this journey of my life I have always attempted to live in the present, anticipate the future and learn from the past. This plan has served me well and surely lingering in the past for long periods is detrimental to one's enjoyment of the present. Still it is nice to look back from time to time and relive an enjoyable moment of the past.

As I look back now, the memories I seek are not always as clear as they have been. A mist often obscures the clear view I really wanted. If I concentrate, I can sometimes part this veil but at other times the past stays clouded.

For this reason I am glad I have my wife's sharp memory as well as that of my brother. I also have my friend Judy who lived on Holland Street where I did and remembers things much more sharply than I do even though we are only one year apart in age. Of course, she is younger.

When I think back I mostly remember the Holland Street days in Clinton, South Carolina. We moved there when I was barely out of infancy and I stayed on that street until I left for college. I had some of my happiest times on Holland Street—and some of my saddest.

What I most like to remember is my childhood with my mother, father, and brother as well as the families of Holland Street. It is always summer when I look back and generally I am nine or ten years old. The mist parts and I am a barefoot boy clad in khaki shorts and a tee shirt running up the street to where the Adairs lived. I can see the four Adair girls—Linda, Judy, Sue, and Trudy; as well as their Adair cousins Mary Keith and June. From up at the top of the street are Mary Ann and Nancy Neighbors and from behind my house are the Trammell boys Billy and Keith.

The sun is warm and spirits are high. For one rare instance we are all in agreement about what games to play. I feel safe and happy with them. Plus in my mind I know there is the security of my house at 203 Holland Street that's waiting for me when my playtime is done.

Tired but elated, I turn and run for home. It seems I am always running in my memories. I am always eager for what is next, for who is next. I race down Holland street and run up to my door and throw it open. I can hear the trusty fan running in the kitchen, plus the sound of two dogs barking in the backyard. My brother is practicing the piano.

I don't stop however until I find my mother. She is in the kitchen and I throw myself into her outstretched arms. Her warmth envelops me and I rest my ear upon her chest and feel the steady, comforting beat of her heart. For this moment in my memory the mists have parted and I am home. It is the safest, most secure place I could ever be.

In the pages of this book, I will try to pierce the mist and find the stories of my past. The focus this time is on the stories I collected during the years 2006, 2007, and 2008. Most of my stories come from my journal and reflect my thoughts and attitudes during that time.

The mists may be gathering but my vision is sure and my thoughts coherent. I look at the past and I see a wealth of tales that I enjoy and hope you do, too.

So open the pages of this book and travel with me once more through the journey of my life.

*Reflections from Route 2006*

## *Look at Your Children and See Immortality*

How amazing is it that you can look at your children and see yourself at their age? My son Sean is my youngest and the one who looks like me—blondish brown hair and blue eyes. He especially looks like me around the eyes. (My oldest son JJ takes after his mother's side of the family—olive complexion, brown hair, and brown eyes.)

Sean also has some of the same traits I have. For one, he would hug a tree. People have told me I would hug a wall so I guess that's where he gets it. If you meet Sean he is more than likely to give you a hug, and I am the same way. My wife and JJ are more reserved in that respect.

When my wife and I first started dating, I would make a trip from Warner Robins, Georgia, to St. Petersburg, Florida, about every other week. I would spend the nights at my brother and his wife's home but would spend the days with Terry and her family. One day, as I was walking towards her house, her father came out to greet me. I gave him a big hug and I thought the poor man was going to die of embarrassment. That's just something he and his family did not do outside their family circle.

A few months after we had started dating I took Terry home to Clinton to meet my friends and relatives, which included just about the entire town. As we got out of the car at my folks' home I could see the cars of relatives who were there to greet us. I left poor Terry standing in the yard as I rushed inside screaming, "She doesn't hug! She doesn't hug!"

My relatives looked at me in amazement and then just laughed. They didn't believe me. They piled en mass out the door and each and every one of them swept Terry up in a bear hug. I will never forget the look of pure desperation that swept over her face. By the time the relatives left, she was exhausted. They had almost hugged her to death—both in saying hello and then later saying goodbye.

With Sean, well, he always greets people with a hug. I think that served him well when he was a youth minister and I think it helps now that he is working with special-needs children. Everyone can use a hug now and then, at least that's my philosophy.

So, if you see Sean or me heading your way brace yourself. Chances are you're going to get hugged. I inherited it from my daddy and Sean inherited it from me. It is known as the "hugging gene." And the Cooper motto as to genes is "if you have it, pass it on."

## *Give Me a Car and Watch Me Drive*

Yesterday I went to Hilton Head, South Carolina, a three-and-a-half-hour drive from my home in Perry, Georgia but that didn't faze me. I had been invited by a book club to give a talk and was ready to go when the alarm clock went off yesterday morning.

Now I enjoy talking to book clubs. Truth is I enjoy talking period. I like to tell stories, talk about movies, and just get to meet and talk with new people. I have always loved to talk. My mother said I talked at an early age because I had so much I wanted to get said.

In addition to liking to talk, I also like to drive. Change that—I love to drive. I like getting behind the wheel of a car and just letting go. I like the thrill of driving and I like the power of driving. When I am in a car, I don't like for anyone else to drive. I want to be in control.

The seven-hour round trip yesterday was like a vacation. On the way to Hilton Head, I ate cheese crackers and peanut butter and drank Diet Coke. I had a new Sugarland CD I had gotten for Christmas, so I was perfectly content. The hours flew by and soon I was there. I wasn't tired. If anything, I was refreshed.

On the way back, I stopped and got a hamburger and fries to eat on the road. Plus, I had a big diet coke to go with it. This time it was the soundtrack from the movie *The Producers* in the CD player. I had seen the movie and the company had sent me the soundtrack as an added bonus. Again the trip was almost instantaneous.

I don't know what it is about driving. It just fascinates me. When we moved to California several years ago, we drove out. I could have kept going except that pesky ocean got in the way. I liked the scenery, the fun of staying in new places, and the adventure of going from coast to coast.

My wife does not like to drive. To her, it's a chore. She is a good driver, but a cautious one. Maybe it's a male thing. Maybe men just like being in control. Or maybe it's just a man's need for speed.

Whatever it is, for me there is just about nothing better than getting behind the wheel of a car and hitting the open road. I do my best thinking when I am driving, and I seem to be smarter when I think behind the wheel. That probably isn't true, but it sure seems that way. I have gotten ideas and solutions that I couldn't get when I was stuck behind a desk.

So God bless the open road and also those brilliant inventors of the automobile. And thank God I live in the age of the automobile. A horse would never have been as much fun.

## *Dance, Everyone, Dance*

Ballroom dancing is everywhere these days. It's on TV, in the movies, and on Broadway. You can't help but being aware of it. People who look like they don't know their right foot from their left are doing the waltz, the rumba, and the two step. It's America's newest pastime and it's sweeping the country.

I am not a smooth dancer. I can get by, but Fred Astaire I am not. When our son got married recently, my wife and I had to dance and the spotlight was on us. You couldn't actually see me counting out the beat but I was pretty shaky. Still in the video of the reception we do look passable doing a regular slow dance.

Now my son JJ, well, that's a different story. He practiced and practiced before the wedding. He and his soon-to-be wife even had their friends coming over to coach them in the dance moves. When he actually had to do the dance steps, I give him an *A* for effort and a *B* for execution. That's probably generous but, hey, he's my son. I will say I don't think he will be winning any dance contests any time soon.

When I was growing up, my mother and several others decided my fifth-grade class should have dance lessons. Our dance instructor was named Mr. Rippy. Mr. Rippy was from out of town and was suave and debonair. He looked the role of a dance instructor.

His assistant was Jane Ray, a local girl who always wanted to leave Clinton and make it on Broadway. She never did. But she did have her moment of glory as Mr. Rippy's dance assistant.

Two afternoons a week we would all head for the Armory in Clinton. We had the same number of girls and boys so we all had partners. My partner was Martha Jane Bryson, my true love. I wasn't a great dancer but Martha Jane was worse than I was. Still they put us through our paces and we learned the box step, the waltz, the

Charleston, the rumba and the cha cha cha. To this day I can remember the basic steps to all those dances.

The magical time was when Mr. Rippy would choose one girl as his partner and Jane would choose one boy as her partner. While the others stood around the dance area the four would dance. When Jane chose me, I learned that with the right partner you are always so much better than you had been before. With her skills taking control, I moved with rhythm and ease around the floor. And, oh, what a feeling that was. Everyone praised our performance.

That memory has stayed with me all these years. I will never be a great dancer but for those few moments at the Clinton Armory when I was eleven years old I was the master of the dance.

So now when I watch *Dancing with the Stars*, I close my eyes and once again Jane Ray and I are dancing. We don't miss a beat. It's showtime and the magic is back.

## *The Roles Have Changed*

Now that I am basically a stay-at-home writer, the roles of responsibilities in my house have changed. My wife gets up and goes to work every day as a school principle while I spend my day at the computer writing articles, reviews, etc. I get up most mornings and kiss her good-bye but there are also days I kiss her from the bed.

During the day I make the bed, wash the dishes, sometimes vacuum, and sometimes go to the store to get items we need. My wife has been on a cooking kick lately and when she cooks I clean up. It works for us and that's what is important.

I was never one of those people who felt the man was king of the castle and the little wife was just there to serve him, though I have known people like that. I've never felt I shouldn't take my turn with the dirty diapers, getting up with the kids, etc. It just seemed fair to me that if you were going to have kids you ought to invest something in their care.

Now don't let me lie to you. I did some things most men didn't, but I didn't do a lot. Most of my time was spent working outside the home and the majority of the house work fell on my wife. She stayed home after the kids were born and only went back to work outside the home after they were in school.

My sons are much more involved in the raising of their kids and the upkeep of their homes. Sean, my youngest son, has two children and he has been much more of a hands-on father than I ever was. He also takes more of an active role in keeping the house clean, washing clothes, etc. He does all the ironing in their house and he is very good at it.

JJ, my oldest, just got married this past summer but he has already plunged into the housework thing. He also is an ironer and does the vacuuming. His wife is the cook in the family but JJ does clean up after they have eaten. He and his wife don't have any kids but I know he will be involved when they arrive.

Do they feel any less male because they help out in these ways? I don't think so. In today's world of two careers in most homes, there just isn't room for male chauvinism. Or at least there isn't room for the rampant male chauvinism that existed in my day and to a worse extent in my father's day.

Today marriage and parenting are more a partnership, an equal thing. That's so much better in the long run. No one feels oppressed all the time. There is a shared concern about money, planning for the future, raising good kids, and on and on. When one spouse feels overcome by events the other spouse is there to help them out.

You can watch the reruns of those old TV shows where the husband sat in the easy chair while the wife vacuumed around him and wonder where those days went. The answer is "with the wind, buddy, with the wind." I don't think we will ever see them blow back into town again.

Today's marriage is a partnership of the best kind and keeps getting better. The secret is in the sharing, and that's honestly the way I think it should be. I am working on being better at it than I have been in the past.

## *Dog Gone*

Last night we got a phone call from our granddaughter, Genna. When my wife answered, Genna said, "Nana, did you hear what happened?"

"Yes, Genna," my wife replied, "your daddy told us that Georgia is not at home."

Georgia is my grandchildren's pet dachshund. She stays in their fenced-in backyard and sometime over the weekend, while Sean and his family were away, she tunneled under the fence and took off.

"Nana knows Walker," Genna hollered to her brother. Then she asked, "Do you think she's alright, Nana?"

"Of course I do," my wife answered. "She has just probably gone to visit some of her friends. She is probably having a great time."

"But she was gone all night," asserted Genna.

"It was probably a sleepover," my brilliant wife replied.

As of now Georgia still has not returned. My son and his wife have looked for her but to no avail. Like many other pets I have known, Georgia has just disappeared. Now I am not giving up. She could certainly reappear at any time. But if she doesn't, I just hope some nice people have found her.

That's one of the problems with having pets. You go into a panic when they go missing. At least that's what always happened to Terry and me when our cat Fluff would disappear. Fluff was an indoor cat. We had had her front paws declawed (I don't think they do that anymore) so she was defenseless in the outdoors.

Still she had that natural instinct to scoot out any outside open door and many were the times she got out and raced away. We would scour the neighborhood and call her name. Sometimes we would find her and sometimes she came back on her own and we would find her at the back door, shivering and waiting to get inside.

Whenever we found her she would look at us as if to ask, "Have you lost your minds? Don't you know I am an indoors cat? Are you completely crazy, insensitive, or what?" Then she would stroll haughtily into the house and ignore us for the next few hours.

I just hope within the next few days Georgia shows up in the same way and lets Sean know she is upset with him. A dog has to do what a dog has to do, but all pets depend on their owners to keep them safe—even from their own instincts.

## *Every Face Is a Memory*

During my last visit to South Carolina I was looking at the faces of people I hadn't seen in years and years. As I studied them, I thought to myself each face is a memory. Yes, each pair of eyes I looked into, each smile that was turned towards me, each voice that spoke my name in recognition—they all brought up memories of life in Clinton, South Carolina, oh so many years ago.

I spent eighteen years living in Clinton while I was growing up. It seemed like forever but as I get older it becomes a smaller and smaller portion of my life. Still the friends I made during those days are ever with me, if often only in spirit. They populate my thoughts and my dreams.

One of my first memories is of Denny. Denny lived next door to me when I was living in the house on Holland Street that my mother and father built. He was a year or so younger than me but we were best buddies. I remember getting up on summer mornings and racing next door to Denny's house so we could play.

Denny lived with his mother, father, uncle and grandmother. His father was an artist of some type and he worked at home. Denny's mother worked downtown. I thought it was just amazing that all five of them lived in one house and got along as well as they did. Three generations under one roof and they all loved and respected each other.

Denny and I stayed friends until he moved to Greenville, South Carolina. I visited him a time or two after he moved but the bond was broken. He still is there in my memory but I haven't seen him in ages. Still, when I see kids running up and down the street shouting and having a great time, the first person I think of is Denny.

Phyllis is another memory. Phyllis and I became good friends because her brother Tommy and I were good friends. Tommy could be moody and sometimes he wanted his friends around and sometimes he didn't. If he was listening to a Kentucky basketball game, he definitely wanted to be left alone to enjoy it. So, I would just hang around and talk with his sister Phyllis.

It was easy to be around her. For one thing she was beautiful, but she was also articulate. She was more sophisticated than any other girl I knew in Clinton, and really didn't care if she was popular or not. A mystique grew up around her because she didn't play the game the other girls in Clinton played.

I don't think she ever dated a high school boy. When she started dating she went straight for the college guys. But even with the college guys she was aloof in that smoky way of hers. She was searching for a special someone but she never found him—at least not yet.

When I last saw her, she had moved back to Clinton after having lived in a variety of places over the years. She is still beautiful, still has the mystique, still doesn't play the Clinton game. I probably knew her as well as anyone did but in retrospect I don't know if I knew her at all.

They all linger inside my mind, these people of my past. Every face is a memory and every memory is a chapter in the book of my life.

## *Happiness Is Just*

She sits at her dining room table and stares into a cup of coffee. She barely has the energy to make it, and certainly doesn't have the energy to drink it. It's as if all of her life force is seeping away. And in her mind she wishes maybe it would.

Through her mind come the strains of an old song. Something about happiness being Joe. She smiles for it is so appropriate. For her happiness is Joe. He has been her happiness for over sixty years and now he has been taken away. Strangely she knows the name of the kidnapper but she can do nothing about it. There is no one she can report this kidnapping to. He was kidnapped by Alzheimer's.

She never thought this day would come when they would be separated, but now she knew he could no longer stay at home. So her daughter and son-in-law had taken him to the facility. What an awful name—the facility. What else would you call it—a home? Not likely. It was a place where he would be cared for and watched over. But what about her? Who would watch over her now that Joe was gone.

In an instant, she begins to rage at God, and then just as quickly she is praying to Him. That's the way it went now; one minute angry and the next minute afraid, and then eventually contrite. She didn't know which way to handle all of this. It's just so confusing.

She hears sounds in the house and she looks around expecting to see him there. She also hears sounds in the night and expects him to be there beside her. Can that be called ghosts? Can there be a ghost when the person who is haunting you isn't dead?

She forces herself to sip the coffee. It tastes bitter, just like her life. It shouldn't be this way. They should have died together in their sleep, or in a car accident, or anything. Together, that's the key word. Together. Not this separateness. She wants to see him right now, wants to hold him, and wants to be held by him.

She presses her hand to her forehead. She wonders if she can bear this. She wonders if she wants to. Would it be a sin to pray to die? But then who would look after Joe? Even if she isn't with him she is still going to make sure he is okay.

She hears the song again in her mind, and she smiles. People try to make happiness so complex. They torture themselves trying to achieve it. They build up fantasies about what would bring happiness. But in her reality, happiness is just a thing called Joe.

## *Some Promises Can't Be Kept*

My father-in-law has Alzheimer's disease. He has had it for nineteen years and it has been a battle from the time he first developed symptoms. He has managed to stay at home until a few days ago. At that point, his wife had done all she could do and she reluctantly told her children he needed care she could not give.

So the family found a wonderful place where he could be cared for around the clock. So far it has worked out pretty good, but it certainly has been hard for the family. One of the big problems was that the children had all promised their father they would take care of him, and that did not include putting him somewhere. They have told me over and over, "I promised him. I promised him."

My answer to this is there are some promises that can't be kept. You keep them for as long as you can but at some point you have to break them. You don't mean to lie when you make the promises but technically you do.

I went through the same thing with my father. As he got older he would say to me often, "Jackie, don't ever put me in a nursing home." And I would assure him I wouldn't. But even as I said it I was adding a codicil, "Not as long as I can keep from it."

In my heart I knew there could be circumstances when my father might have to be put in a nursing home. Thankfully he never reached that point but he could have, and I would have. I could lie and say I wouldn't have but I know in my heart that if it had been necessary I would.

From all of this, I have learned to never ask my children for such promises. It isn't fair to them to do that. When such promises are made it can be heart wrenching to have to break them. And then there is the guilt—there is always the guilt.

Dealing with elderly parents is not an easy thing to do. In most cases the children all work, and have other responsibilities. The parent(s) usually do not want to go into assisted living or nursing-home care. In the case of my father, he was living in South Carolina and I live in Georgia. Once, he called me and told me I needed to move to South Carolina to take care of him and his wife.

I tried to explain that I had a job and couldn't do that. Then I mentioned the possibility of them moving to Perry, Georgia. He told me not to be silly, that he would never leave South Carolina. He had been born there and he would die there. And he did. He died in his home and never had to be moved to a nursing home—but if he had had to, well, that's what I would have done.

We make promises a lot of times because they are demanded. We make them to give our parents peace of mind. We make them for a variety of reasons. But there are some promises that can't be kept.

We all have miles to go before we sleep, and there are some promises we just can't keep.

## *The Best Book Festival Ever*

One of the best parts of being a writer is getting to go to book festivals. Prior to having my first book published I didn't know such events even existed. But after I had a book in print I was contacted by an organization sponsoring a festival and invited to attend. I went, and now I am addicted to them.

The best thing about book festivals is getting to meet other authors. I have always been in awe of people who write and getting to know some of them personally has been a wonderful treat for me. When I meet some of my idols I kind of detach myself from the reality of who they are. That's the only way I can stand and converse with them without behaving like a blubbering idiot. Then when I get home and think about who I have actually spoken with, I am amazed. I play the conversation over and over in my mind and have a ball with it.

I was particularly happy to get an invitation to the South Carolina Book Festival this year. There are two reasons why this event is special. First, I am a South Carolinian by birth so this was a homecoming in a sense. Second, I attended this festival last year so I knew how nice everyone associated with it is. These people treat the authors like royalty and stay pleasant and attentive the entire time.

My wife and I drove up to Columbia, South Carolina, on Thursday even though the festival didn't kick off until Friday. I had agreed to talk to two of my friend Bob Lamb's writing classes at the University of South Carolina. Bob is the author of *Atlanta Blues*. His classes are small and the students were very attentive when I spoke. Then they read some of their work and that was exciting to hear.

On Friday afternoon I went to Sumter, South Carolina, for a book signing at one of the malls. I was told there was not much traffic in the mall that day because a writer was speaking to the Friends of the Library. The writer turned out to be Mary Alice Monroe, who was also attending the South Carolina Book Festival. Mary Alice is the author of several books, the latest being *Sweetgrass*.

Mary Alice drew a crowd in Sumter and also a crowd at the festival. In one of the first author signings, I was stationed between her and Sandra Brown. People were lined up in droves, and they weren't coming to see me. I did manage to bask in the reflected glow of "celebritydom" emanating from both Mary Alice and Ms Brown.

One person I was looking forward to seeing was Anne Rivers Siddons. I had met Ms. Siddons and her husband several years ago and was impressed with both of them. Sadly Ms. Siddons was felled by the flu and was unable to come to Columbia.

I did get a chance to finally meet Cassandra King in person. I had interviewed her by phone for a radio program a few years back when her book *The Sunday Wife* was released. I had read the book and found it to be enjoyable and insightful. I was also interested in her because she is married to my all-time-favorite writer Pat Conroy.

Between the time I interviewed King on the radio and her appearance at the South Carolina Book Festival I had met Pat Conroy. So now I was able to talk with Ms. King again. She is a very down-to-earth person who is just as friendly as can be. Once you engage her in conversation you're able to relax completely.

Every author I met at the South Carolina Book Festival was interesting from Ken McCullough to James Huston to Bob Meyer to Jennifer Cruisie. And the list goes on and on. My wife says that authors are more down-to-earth than actors and I think that's true. Or maybe I have just been blessed to meet some of the very nicest around.

The South Carolina Book Festival featured panel discussions, book signings, and the chance to meet and greet in a one-on-one setting. It was the best festival I have ever attended, and I look forward to going back again and again.

## *Just in Case*

How much better off this world would be if we all just learned to love and look after each other. It shouldn't be that difficult. Children do it every day, like my grandchildren Genna, age six, and Walker, age three. They are brother and sister and they truly love each other—more so than I remember my children doing at that age, and more so I know than my brother and I did at that age.

Genna is very protective of Walker and is constantly checking on him to see if he is alright. Walker is just as concerned with her wellbeing. Sure, they argue from time to time but all children do. These are children not saints.

Anyway, recently my wife was in Moultrie, Georgia, taking care of them while their parents were tied up with work projects. When it came time to go out for lunch my wife told Walker he needed to go to the bathroom before they got in the car. He said he was fine but Genna was concerned. "He has been having accidents," she said, "and has had to go to timeout."

Still Walker insisted he was fine and off they went to the fast food place. By the time they got there Walker was desperate to find a bathroom. He made it—almost. He did show signs of an accident. This upset him and this in turn upset Genna.

The next day when they again started to go find a place to eat Genna went into the back of the house and came out with her purse. As my wife was seatbelting them into the car Genna turned to Walker and said, "Don't worry, Walker. I brought some extra panties in case you need them."

"Panties or underpants?" asked Walker, looking confused.

"Your underpants," Genna answered. "You know, just in case you need them."

Sure enough she opened her purse and there was a hairbrush, some lip gloss, and a pair of her brother's underpants. She wasn't going to let him be upset again, not if she could help it.

We should all be blessed with having someone that concerned with our well-being. Sometimes it takes seeing things through the eyes of a child to make us aware of our own shortcomings. Maybe we should all do that something special, go that extra mile, make that extra effort for someone we love. We should have their back in the event something happens.

We should all pack that extra pair of underpants—just in case.

## *Fear Itself*

Some people are basically paranoid, and that description pretty much suits me. In today's age I find a lot of things to be paranoid about. It's easy. Just pick up the newspaper or turn on TV and you will find a check list of possibilities that can turn you gray overnight.

Look up in the sky and spot a cloud. Is it a possible tornado? Or go to the beach, then you can worry about sharks or tsunamis. Somewhere there's a bunch of killer bees ready to sting you to death. The article I read about them said they were generally harmless unless you aggravate them. I guess that means you are safe unless you call them names—or buzz off key.

Honestly, just going to your fast food place for a snack can put the fear of God into you. I headed out the other day with chili on my mind. Then I remembered that story I had read about possible mad cow disease being found in Alabama. That state is next door so that put a chill on my chili.

So I decided maybe some chicken nuggets would be tasty. Wait a minute, I thought, what about bird flu? Do chickens get bird flu, or are they all tested before they end up in those huge trucks I see with cages piled on top of cages? Better stick with a salad. Then when I got home I turned on TV and there was some guy talking about too many pesticides being used on lettuce.

My wife is a vegetarian, has been for years. She says she never felt better and urges me constantly to convert. So far I have withstood her pleas. I love steaks and hamburgers and chili. How could I live without my weekly intake of spaghetti! Watching my wife eating her salads and vegetables doesn't do it for me. Those are side dishes not the main course.

I really think we have to just live our lives and pray for the best. We can only hide from the realities for so long. I had a friend whose parents were both sickly people. He worried all his life about them dying, and you know what? They both outlived him. He was killed in a car wreck in his early thirties and both his parents are still alive. All that time of worry was just wasted.

Still I live in fear of the unknown. My poor wife has to call me when she leaves school each day so I will know she is on her way home. I also check in on my kids every day just to make sure things are all right. I just need that daily reassurance they are doing okay. I used to just have to only worry about my wife and two sons. Now I also have two daughters-in-law and two grandchildren I have to monitor.

Franklin Roosevelt said, "The only thing we have to fear is fear itself." Well, he didn't know how my mind operates. I fear everything *and* fear itself. I know that uses up a lot of energy and I wish I could stop, but I think I am just programmed to be a little insecure about things.

My preacher ended her sermon last week with this story about a woman who was just sure her home was going to be burglarized. She told her husband over and over that this was going to occur. Finally one night they did hear a noise in their home. The husband got up to check and sure enough there was a burglar standing in their den.

The husband looked at the burglar, who seemed to be searching for an escape route, and said, "Could you wait here a minute. I want to get my wife. She'll be so excited to see you. She's been expecting you for years."

That says so much about a lot of us. We profess to be optimistic about the future but we are always waiting for the next shoe to drop. There is just something in our DNA that whispers, "Watch out. Things are going too good."

We have to fight these feelings, fight these fears. We have to trust in God and our abilities to overcome whatever faces us. This is not an easy thing to do but it is something we have to do.

## *Goodbye Was Long Ago*

A few days ago I ran into someone I used to work with in one of my early jobs. One of my first questions was to ask about our old colleague Ann. There was a moment of hesitation and then this person answered, "Ann died two weeks ago. She had a stroke."

As I digested this fact, I thought back to when I first met Ann. We had an immediate rapport and worked together easily. After a few weeks she asked if I would like to come to work for her. As strange as it seems now, I hesitated because I had never had a female boss before. I actually hadn't been in the work force long so my experience with employers was not vast. Still all the supervisors I had had up to that time had been other males. I thought about it and then decided what the heck. I liked her. She seemed to like me, so why not. I requested a transfer and Ann became my boss—and my mentor.

We did have a great working relationship. She was the type of boss who encouraged her employees to be their best, and because she was good and fair you worked extra hard for her. Plus we became good friends. She met my wife and I got to know her daughter. Ann was a widow so her daughter and her family were everything to her.

During our lunch hour Ann was always looking for a group to play bridge. I quickly became a part of that group. We played bridge and laughed and talked and had a wonderful time. It was one of the best work situations I ever had. It just didn't last long enough. After a couple of years, Ann decided I needed to expand my knowledge of the workplace and had me enroll in a program that would give me more experience.

After a year in another area I got a job in California and moved my family out there. We stayed for two years, and during that time Ann and I lost touch. After I returned to Georgia, I meant to look her up but didn't, and by the time I did she had retired. I asked a mutual friend why he didn't let me know about Ann's retirement dinner. He said that Ann had made out the guest list and only included her closest friends.

Those words really stung me as I had thought Ann and I were very close. I had considered her one of my best friends even though we hadn't seen each other in a while. But I guess she hadn't felt the same way.

I ran into Ann one day in the post office and we spoke and chatted about life when we worked together. She acted like we were still good friends but I couldn't get out of my mind that she hadn't included me in that dinner list. Maybe that was petty on my part but my feelings had been hurt. We parted with those words about how we would have to get together, but I knew we wouldn't. I said goodbye to her and that was it.

That was seven years ago, and now that goodbye is finally final. There will be no chance to clear up the hard feelings I had about being excluded from her retirement dinner. There will be no chance to rekindle the friendship we once had. Life goes by at a rapid pace. If we need to make contact with someone to clear up a misunderstanding we need to do it now—today!

I grieve for the loss of Ann today, but even though I didn't know it I said goodbye to her a long time ago.

## *Truth Be Told*

Were you raised to believe that honesty is the best policy? I was. It was one of those truisms my parents imparted to me. Although, I believed it for maybe a week. Then it dawned on me that telling the truth can hurt someone's feelings, can get you into trouble, and can make for an unhappy world.

The first time I realized honesty was not always the best policy was when I was playing up the street with the Neighbors girls. They were my neighbors but they were also named Neighbors—Mary Ann and Nancy Neighbors. I guess I was six or seven when this happened. I got aggravated with Mary Ann for some reason and I pinched her. I didn't pinch her hard, just a little pinch on her arm. Mary Ann didn't yell or cry or anything.

A little later her mother hollered out the door and asked if we were playing nicely. Mary Ann answered that I had pinched her. Her mother just said for me not to do that again. I guess she could see Mary Ann wasn't in pain.

When I asked Mary Ann why she had told her mother I had pinched her, when it hadn't even hurt, she replied that she had to tell the truth. That was lightbulb number one telling me that truth is not always the best thing.

Later in high school, I had a friend named Jean who was blunt to the extreme. If you asked her about something, she would tell you point blank. I remember one time I had gone out for the basketball team. Being non-athletic it was a struggle to even keep up at practice.

One day Jean came by the gym and watched me at practice. Later we were talking and she said that I was embarrassing to watch. Now I knew how bad I was, but I didn't need a friend telling me how bad I was. The light bulb went on again and I knew this truth thing wasn't all it had been cracked up to be.

Years later when I got married my new bride asked me if a certain dress made her look fat. Well, I was young and stupid and wanted my wife to be reed thin. Still I was not dropped on my head as a baby, so I replied of course not. If I had said it did, my wife probably would have starved herself into anorexia.

So, no, telling the truth is not always the best policy. Sometimes a little tact and a little white lie can go a long, long way in keeping relationships good and families happy. Remember the movie *Liar, Liar* with Jim Carey? That movie stands as a prime example of what can happen when you are dedicated to truth.

Even George Washington probably used a little tact now and then. Maybe he didn't exactly say he cut down the cherry tree. Maybe he said he fell on it and it broke. Sounds good to me.

## *What's Faith Got to Do with It?*

When I was growing up in Clinton, South Carolina, I attended the First Baptist Church. Everybody on Holland Street did. We were all staunch Baptists and most of our friends and acquaintances were too. It wasn't necessarily that we all thought the same way or even had the same views on God and religion, the First Baptist Church was just the place where my father's family had worshipped for years—and so we went there.

When my wife and I married, we were wed in a Baptist Church, the one she attended in St. Petersburg, Florida. She was Baptist, I was Baptist, so you would think we would attend a Baptist church. Nope, we turned Methodist. Something inside us told us we just weren't meant to be Baptists any more. We didn't have an argument with the Baptists, we just had an amicable divorce.

When my wife and I had children, we made sure they attended Sunday school and church regularly at the Perry Methodist Church. The kids seemed to appreciate the services and both joined the church early on. We looked into the future and saw a long line of Coopers attending Methodist churches. Didn't happen.

Both of my sons and their families attend non-denominational churches. They like singing music that's not found in hymnals. They like having people playing musical instruments on the platform. They like having song leaders. They like more informality. They like a less strict dress code. They like everything about it. When they visit us and attend church with us you can tell they feel stifled by my wonderful more orderly form of worship.

I like singing hymns. I like the sound of the organ playing. I like hearing a choir sing a cantata. I like a formal order of worship. I like wearing clothes that are dressier than jeans. I like everything about my more formal way of worshipping. And when I go to church with my sons I feel completely out of place. I am getting better but I still don't know the songs they sing, and I keep looking for the choir.

I am sure my poor old father, who never understood us turning Methodist, is spinning in his grave. He would never have felt comfortable in this kind of service. He might have attended just to be nice, but he wouldn't have liked it.

My opinion is live and let live. The fact that they are going to church is the important thing, and even more importantly that they have faith. Faith is the key to everything in my opinion. It is what gets you through the bad times and makes you appreciate the good times. All of the ins and outs of churches and church people are unimportant in the long run, but you gotta, gotta have faith.

I like the feeling that someone higher is in control, because I certainly am not. I can barely make the necessary decisions in my life, much less take care of the world. So yes faith is everything to me. It is my cornerstone.

I will be Methodist till the day I die but it surely isn't something I would ever want to force on my family. We all have different needs in order to find our path, I am just grateful there is such a variety being offered.

## *Living in a Black-and-White World*

Back in my childhood days a lot movies were made in black and white. The "colored" movies were special—and, no, I did not grow up in the Stone Age. TV was also in black and white for the most part, and I can well remember when we got our first colored TV set. I never was that crazy about black and white. I preferred to see the whole rainbow of colors.

However in this day and age, there are still the rare movies that are made in black and white. Movie auteurs seem to think this gives the movie a gravitas that a "technicolor" film would not have. I don't buy that, but if they do and certain segments of the audience do, well, more power to them.

But just like I don't get people's nostalgia over black-and-white movies, I don't get technology. I am what's known as "technically challenged." I can do some basic things with computers and other electronic equipment but get technical on me and I am lost. Both of my sons however are whizzes at the computer, etc stuff.

They grew up on computers and gameboys and other electronic fun. They are the ones who insisted we have a VCR. My problem was I could never get the thing programmed right. The boys would always have to step in. Then they insisted I get a computer, and they set it up for me.

The problem is they grew up and left home, and left me with this equipment that's Greek to me. I never did conquer the knowledge of the computer set-up and I never could completely program my VCR. Then they decided I needed a Tivo.

For those of you who do not own a Tivo, or something like it, it records TV shows for you effortlessly. You tell it what you like and then sit back and relax. It does it day after day, month after month, and year after year. I love it. Honestly I do.

I have had my Tivo for about two years now and it has always worked perfectly. But about a month ago it began to skip some shows I wanted taped. I called the Tivo people and they walked me through some adjustments but it didn't get fixed. Then my youngest son came home and worked on it and it seemed to be fine *except* it records some shows in black and white.

Now you see where this is all going. I am back to the dark ages, watching TV without color. I still love my Tivo and don't want a new one (I paid the one-time lifetime service charge). So here I sit watching *American Idol* in glorious black and white.

But you know what, I am beginning to appreciate the glory of a black-and-white world. There are shades of black and white that almost approach the variety of colors. And when I am watching a serious drama I don't need the distraction of color. As Jack Webb used to say on *Dragnet* so many years ago, "I just want the facts ma'am, just the facts." Well, black and white gives you the facts of the show.

Eventually, I will break down and get a new machine and go back to my all color world, but for now it is a nice diversion. Plus sometimes we have to rough it to appreciate what we are missing.

## *On the Radio*

When I was growing up in Clinton, South Carolina, one of my best friends, Georgia Young, and I had a radio show. How or why we had a radio show is one of the great mysteries of the universe but we decided we wanted one so we got one. She and I convinced the station manager at our local station that a high school show was just what his station needed.

Many years later I decided that I wanted to do a one-hour radio show about movies. Somehow, I convinced the local radio station manager that this was something his station needed, and I got it. I enjoyed this one even more than I did the high school show, because by now I had done some television work and radio is so much more relaxed than television.

Radio is also a much more intimate medium than television. You are in people's homes, in their cars, at their workplace, even where they play—you are everywhere. Plus people can make you anything they want you to be. You are a disembodied voice and you could look like Brad Pitt or Gilbert Gottfried.

Recently, I have concentrated on being on television. I didn't have an idea for a radio show, and contented myself with making guest appearances on other people's shows. I pop up on the local *Kenny B and Jami G Show* from time to time. And believe it or not I am the entertainment correspondent for *Dave Sturgeon's Show* in Canada—yes, Canada!

A few months ago, I was the guest on *Cover to Cover*, a monthly program about books on Georgia Public Radio. The host of that show is a Britisher named St. John Flynn (St. John is pronounced *sinjin*.). Anyway, I had a great time doing that show and felt that our two personalities made for good conversation. Other people commented on how compatible we were as a team.

That started me thinking about a show I had listened to many years ago. It was on National Public Radio on Friday mornings. Bob Edwards, who was the host of *Morning Edition*, would have a five-minute conversation with Red Barber each week. Barber was one of the greatest sports announcers ever and he and Bob would discuss different aspects of sports. Now I know next to nothing about sports, but I loved their conversations and I tuned in for their talks religiously.

Using this as a guide, I suggested to St. John that he and I do a similar type show but about entertainment. He liked the idea and starting May 5 *Fridays with Jackie* will air on all Georgia Public Radio stations.

I am not giving up my day job as a film critic on our local NBC affiliate, but I am happy to be returning to radio. It's where I started alongside my friend Georgia so many years ago, and now I am broadcasting from the state of Georgia. There's a message in there somewhere.

## *When I Grow Up/Retire*

Time certainly has a way of changing your view on things. For example, I remember being asked when I was small what I wanted to be when I grew up. I don't actually remember my answer but when I grew up the decision as to what I did was based on a lot of factors and not just what I wanted. I had to think how I would support a wife and children rather than just what would make me happy.

I was lucky in that all the time I was working at my full time job (personnel manager for the Air Force Reserve), I was also able to do things I liked to do on the side. I wrote articles for newspapers, was on radio and TV, and eventually began to write books. But as time passed the question people began to ask was what I was going to do when I retired.

In this day and age, people are living longer and being healthier longer. That means that most of us can plan to be retired at some point in our life, and we will hopefully be able to do those things we always wanted to do. I know people who have started second careers as painters, woodworkers, writers, and other "fun" jobs.

I think really we are the first generation to be able to plan to do work in retirement that will make us happy. My father's generation just wanted to be able to retire period. My father worked hard jobs for long hours so when he did finally retire he was tired. All he wanted to do in retirement was not work. He didn't want to take up a second career, no thank you very much. He just wanted to sit around the house, go to a ballgame now and then, visit with his kids, and that was it. He was happy basically doing nothing.

Other people I have talked with who retire and don't have anything to do are miserable. They say the days have no purpose and just stretch out forever in front of them. I am sure they could find something that would make them happy but they tell me they don't have a clue as to what it is.

My brother is retired. He was an English teacher and retired from the school system. Today he stays busy substitute teaching. He says it is good for him to have something to do that gets him out of the house. On days when he isn't called in to sub he makes sure he has some other activity planned. He is divorced and lives alone so I am sure it's lonesome when he doesn't have something planned to do.

Of course one requirement of doing your dream activity when you retire is having enough money to live on while you pursue these second careers. With companies scaling back on retirement programs and health costs going through the roof, having enough money is not always a given. It takes some hard planning.

Still it is nice to know that today most people can count on a second act to life. The first fifty years may be for security and the second fifty for fun. Sounds like a winner doesn't it? Here's hoping all of you will have that second fifty and it will be full of all the things you once said you wanted to do when you grew up.

## *One-Upmanship*

The art of selling books is not something I have, or even particularly want to have. I like to write books. I like to talk about what I have written. I like meeting people who have read or want to read what I have written. I do not like the process of selling books to people, but this is a necessary evil when you become a writer with a published book.

I probably do thirty or more book signings each year. These can come in the form of after-dinner talks; addresses to book clubs, garden clubs, social clubs, etc., or actual gatherings of authors for one event or another. This past weekend I talked to the American Association of University Women on Saturday and then attended an arts festival at Henderson Village just south of Perry on Sunday.

At the AAUW I had lunch with the group and then gave a talk. This was followed by the chance for them to buy my books and get them autographed. I'm always amused when someone asks me which one of the three books they should buy. I honestly don't have an answer to that question and usually reply they are all like my children and I love them equally.

I do add that if they are going to give the book as a gift it is best to get a hardback (*Halfway Home*), and if they intend to read all of my books they should start with the first one which is *Journey of a Gentle Southern Man*. But all of the books stand alone so you can hop into any of them and not be confused.

At the arts festival at Henderson Village I was set up in a gazebo with Lee Ann Tuggle. Lee Ann is from Perry (like me) and has written a children's book titled *Go Fish*. We shared a table and had a nice conversation as we set up our book displays. Then we waited for the customers to come.

There were not a lot of people milling around as it was a dreary overcast day and it looked like it was going to pour down rain any minute. Finally one guy did stroll up to where we were sitting. I was excited when he addressed me by name and said he had hoped I would be at Henderson Village. I knew this was going to be an easy sell of at least one book and maybe all three.

He offered his hand and said he had heard me on the radio Friday morning. My first segment of *Fridays with Jackie* had aired on all the Georgia Public Radio stations so I was very pleased to learn someone had been listening.

Then he added, "You mentioned a book on that show by some writer in Atlanta."

"Yes, it was *When Light Breaks* by Patti Callahan Henry," I informed him.

"That's it. I think my wife would really like that book. Is it in bookstores?" he asked.

When I assured him that it was, he said they would sure get it, and off he went.

As he departed, the sky opened up and a downpour started. Lee Ann and I gathered up our books and ran for our cars. The day was over.

Final tally of books sold—Jackie K. Cooper: 0, Patti Callahan Henry: 1. I had been one-upped in my own booth.

## *I Never Sang for My Father*

When I was in either the fifth or sixth grade, I had a good boy soprano voice. It was so good that the music teacher, Dr. Nielsen, selected me to sing a solo in the state competition. The song was "If with All Your Heart You Truly Seek Him" and it had some high notes in it. I was very flattered to be selected but scared silly at the thought of having to sing in a competition.

The competition was held in Columbia, South Carolina, and all of us kids were taken there on a school bus. If parents wanted to go, they had to provide their own transportation. At that time, I don't think we even owned a car so there was no way my mother could go. I remember telling her how scared I was and she told me just to sing it like I was singing it for her. And that's what I did. I stood up, got her image in my mind and sang it just for her.

Now the great thing would be if I could say I sang like an angel that day, but I didn't. I think I actually cracked on that high note at the end. Still I did alright and got through it without embarrassing myself.

The important thing was my mother believed in me, and whenever she did come to hear me perform or get an award or whatever, I knew when I was on stage I was doing it for her. And I continued to have that feeling even after she died.

My father was a good man. Everybody loved him and he basically loved everybody. Still he was not much a part of my life. Now that doesn't mean I didn't love him, I did. It was just that we didn't talk much, and we never talked about important things. From the time my mother died his goal was just to get me raised with as few problems as possible.

That means he never talked to me about getting good grades. He never talked to me about staying out of trouble with girls, drugs, etc.

He never talked about me going to college or choosing a career field. I was on my own in those areas.

Now was this a good way to parent? No. But I guess it was the only way he knew. He and his father had never had a relationship like I wanted. He told me one time he was afraid of his father, and having known him I could see why. He was not an overly friendly man. Still I wish my father had made the effort to go beyond what his father was in regards to our relationship.

After I was grown and would visit my father, he began to tell people what a good father he was. He would repeat it over and over like some kind of mantra. And when he asked if I agreed, I would smile and agree. But inside I was denying it. He was a good man. He was not a good father.

When I graduated from college, my father and my stepmother came to the ceremonies. I was president of the class and so had to make a small speech. When I did it, I thought about my mother and I felt certain she was listening. As I recall my father never mentioned my speech; he just said he was glad I had graduated.

Everyone needs someone to "sing" to and for. For so many years, it was my mother. Now it is my wife, my sons, and my grandkids. I have had a blessed life in so many ways. One of my regrets is that I never sang for my father. It was his loss but now I see it also was mine.

## *Out of the Mouth of Babes*

Last weekend my wife and I traveled to Moultrie, Georgia, for the annual dance recital in which our granddaughter Genna participates. The recital was actually in Cairo, Georgia, but we went to my son Sean's house and rode the rest of the way with him and our grandson Walker. Genna and her mother Paula had gone on ahead.

Terry had brought flowers to present to Genna and a coloring book and crayons for Walker. She thought he might want to use them while watching the performances as they tend to be a bit long for someone his age. When we all got into Sean's car and started out, Walker turned to me and said, "I didn't like the present. I don't know how to color good."

Walker is four and has been encouraged to speak his mind. Sean and Paula do not spank their children so they are always telling them to use their words. Instead of hitting his sister, he is encouraged to tell her to stop doing what she is doing or to go away. This makes for very verbal children, but one's that don't hit each other a lot.

Later at the recital, Walker did take out the coloring book and colors and with his Nana's help did a pretty good job of coloring. I almost started coloring myself. This was another one of those three-and-a-half hour dance recitals—and that's way too long in my book. Genna was actually only in two numbers but they were spaced out accordingly so that you virtually had to be there for the entire thing.

Sean did try to get her to leave after her last number but she said she couldn't miss the curtain call. "They have brainwashed my daughter," he said. I tended to agree with this since she was on the back row when the curtain calls were made and could barely be seen. I thought they would parade all of them down front for a wave to the audience/parents. But no, the big kids blocked every one of the smaller ones.

Afterwards we waited for Paula to go backstage and get Genna. When they came outside Genna was madder than a wet hen. "What's the problem?" I asked her.

"Mama gave me the worst present possible," she answered. "She gave me this" and with that she held up a beautiful hairbrush with sparkles on the back. "I hate hairbrushes," she added.

In truth Genna has beautiful red hair but she also has a sensitive scalp and doesn't like having her hair brushed. I assume Paula was trying to encourage more hairbrushing by giving her the jeweled one.

When we got back to Moultrie, Genna was still in a funk and was sent to her room. At six years old she does tend to get a little dramatic. She did manage to tearfully thank us for the flowers. I guess they were okay, but she was still having problems with that brush.

On the way back home my wife and I were talking about her saying how much she didn't like the present. We decided it was good she was honest about it. My wife said she was the type of person growing up who would never have said she disliked anything her parents bought for her. But she did admit there were some gifts that she really didn't like. I, on the other hand, usually said what I thought and let the chips fall where they might.

Now that we know about hairbrushes and coloring books we will avoid them in the future as gifts for Genna and Walker. We will respect their likes and dislikes. I don't advocate children being rude, but I am a supporter of their being honest.

We may not like the honest reactions we get, but we will be all the wiser for it. I know this may contradict my opinion about honesty stated earlier, but now we are talking about children—little children. As adults we should be able to live with their honesty, at least until they become teenagers.

## *Old Fashioned*

Today my wife and I celebrate thirty-six years of marriage. And, yes, on my next birthday I will be one hundred and two years old! My wife said to me this morning, "How can we have been married for thirty-six years when I only feel about thirty-eight years old?" All I know is I want there to be thirty-six more years of married bliss ahead of us.

I remember clearly when we got married. I was scared to death. I wanted to be married but I was afraid of what would happen if I weren't happy. I had been raised to think divorce was a no-no so I figured if I got married and it wasn't right then I was stuck. But as I was standing at the altar in the church waiting for my bride to walk in, I decided right then and there if I was unhappy then I would get out of it. That eased my mind and I have been happy ever since.

I know that sounds a little loony but my theory actually became "plan the divorce and then you will have a happy marriage." I am just a person who has to have an escape clause, even if I would never use it except in the most extreme circumstances.

My wife and I got married and had our children after we were married. Now there is a revolutionary concept. In today's world, especially among celebrities. It seems getting the marriage license is not a necessity. Angelina and Brad, Tom and Katie—the requirement for being wed before having children is passé.

What adults do is their business, but what adults do to children is another matter. I could care less what consenting adults decide to do with their lives. But when they make decisions that impact their children, then I think they should think twice. In most of the country, the term "illegitimate" is not used as commonly as it once was. That doesn't, however, mean it is gone forever, and it doesn't mean it couldn't return with a vengeance.

Children have a hard enough time as it is. They don't need some added stigma or mark against them. They need every break their parents and society can give them. To have their parents choose not to make their union legal is just asking too much of a child.

And why not get married. If a couple are in love and are compatible, and especially if they want to have children, why not make it legal? I know that it meant something to me all those years ago to stand up in front of God, family, and friends and make a commitment. Now from today's perspective I wouldn't change a thing.

I have heard there cannot be anything worse than a bad marriage, but I can vouch for the fact that there is nothing better than a good one. I honestly cannot imagine being single again. Marriage is definitely the right state for me.

So call me old fashioned, but I am truly celebrating the past thirty-six years. It is a celebration of love, fidelity, family, and friendship. In one word it is *everything*!

## *Life Is a Vacation*

It's summertime and that means it is time to think about vacationing again. Should my wife and I go to the beach, the mountains, to visit the kids, to visit the in-laws? What are we to do? My answer is nothing at all. I am the type of person whose idea of a vacation is doing the same old same old.

My youngest son and his wife just got back from a few days in Vegas. Then he went to a seminar at Hilton Head and took the wife and kids with him. Next they are going to Myrtle Beach for five days. Wow! Whose son is he? The answer is his mother's. She loves vacations. The longer the better. I am a three-day man. A day to get there, a day to be there, and a day to get home.

My wife says it takes at least two days before she unwinds so if we come home the next day she doesn't feel like she's had a vacation. Me, I start thinking about what I'm missing back home and I start to tense up. I can just imagine how many e-mails are filling my mailbox, and how many interview possibilities I'm foregoing. I miss getting my mail at the mailbox and making my daily run to the Seven Eleven to get my *USA Today* along with my Diet Coke and cheese crackers.

These sound like humdrum things I know, but I like that routine way of living and I don't need a vacation to get away from it. Doing the ordinary things in life is my form of a vacation and I don't have to rent a motel room and eat out to enjoy it.

My brother and I were talking this past week and he and I feel exactly the same way about this vacation thing. He said he had never been on a vacation when he didn't long to get back home, and this is from a man who has toured Europe many, many times. He said he always gets excited about the idea of going on a trip, but as soon as the journey starts he begins to wish it was time to go home.

My wife and I took a trip to Greece several years ago. I actually won the trip on a quiz show so I couldn't exactly say I didn't want to go. So there we were sailing out of Athens for a cruise up and down the Mediterranean, with stops at the various Greek isles. It was a ten-day cruise and I wondered how I was going to keep from going crazy.

Just like clockwork, after day three I was thinking constantly about going home. I wanted to watch American television. I wanted to be among my own friends and neighbors. I wanted to eat American food. The islands were beautiful, as was the Mediterranean Sea, but once I had seen the sights, I had seen the sights.

This year my wife will want to go on vacation again. I can see it in her eyes. I know I will capitulate and try to muster some enthusiasm. But all the while I am off on holiday my soul will be yearning for the routine and mundane life I left behind in Perry, Georgia.

## *In Praise of Red-Headed Girls*

My granddaughter Genna has red hair and she loves it. She ought to since we tell her constantly how beautiful it is. We also stress that only special people have red hair and having blue eyes with the red hair is even more rare. She likes it when we say these things. Heck, she eats it up—and who wouldn't?

One reason we brag on her hair so much is that shortly after our red-headed grandbaby was born I took a survey of sorts of people with red hair. Just about 100 percent of the women I asked about their red hair said they hated it when they were growing up but liked it now. They said when they were growing up their hair made them feel different, and at an early age no one wants to feel they are different.

So we wanted to stress to Genna from an early age on that having red hair was special—not different in a bad way. So far it seems to have worked. She will tell people she likes her hair, and that's a good thing. She also likes for my wife to roll and curl it when there is a special occasion. This was the case this past weekend when she was gong to be in a relative's wedding. My wife Terry washed and curled it and even put flowers in Genna's hair.

When she was completely styled, she came downstairs and met our *oohs* and *ahhs*. Even Walker, her four-year-old brother, told her how pretty she looked. She took it all with serenity being the princess that she is. She was the picture of composure as she went off to the wedding, and still looked great when she returned although the flowers were missing from her hair and it was hanging loose and not upswept. You can only be beautiful for so long.

I think children need to be praised continually. They need to feel special and cherished. Marlo Thomas has a new book out called *The Right Words at the Right Time, Volume 2*. One of the stories in the book concerns a little girl named Jane. Now an adult, this woman wrote that as a child she was called "Plain Jane" and was even told by her parents she was homely. Can you believe that?

Her idol was Roger Williams, the pianist. She thought he was the greatest, so when she heard he would be close to her hometown giving a concert she begged her parents to take her. And they did. Jane got all dressed up in her best dress and even curled and combed her hair.

Jane said the concert was everything she hoped it would be, and afterwards they announced Williams would sign autographs. Jane got in the line and finally made it to the table where Williams was seated. She said he looked up and said to her, "Well, hello, pretty girl."

That was it. That was what she needed to hear. She said it changed her life because someone saw something in her that was pretty. She never forgot it and in the years to come it gave her confidence.

So if you see a red-haired little girl tell her how pretty her hair is. And anyone else you meet, pull out a compliment for them. We hear enough of the bad; let's try using some of the good.

## *God Bless America*

As I write this, it is July 4, 2006. It is the most patriotic holiday of the year and a time when we reflect back on where our country has been, where it is, and where it is going. It is a day of happiness and a day of sadness, a time of hope and a time of fear. I have seen some terrible things in my lifetime and I am always fearful of what else might occur.

I have lived through a lot of wars in my life. The first I really remember was the Korean conflict. I had a cousin who married a man who was in the military. He was sent to Korea and she came home to Clinton to live while he was away. Listening to Patricia talk about Marshall and his involvement in that war made it more personal for me. Then when it was over and he came home, it was a time of great celebrating within my family.

Next came Vietnam. It was very personal to me as I was in the military during that time and lived with the reality that on any given day I could get orders to go there. That never happened for me, but it happened to a lot of my friends. They got the news and they went. Luckily all but one of them came home.

The scars I saw from that war among my friends were mostly emotional rather than physical. I saw a lot of marriages break up because of Vietnam. Spouses who were not used to making all the decisions about family life had to take on that role while they were alone. Then when their partner returned and wanted to reassume those duties, well, it caused conflict. And some of these conflicts couldn't be overcome.

Next came the first Gulf War and now the second incursion into the Middle East. I hate the thought of families being ripped apart because of this war, and I pray for and fear for every person assigned to Iraq or Afghanistan. But I don't discuss the politics of the war because I am conflicted in my thoughts.

When my two sons were growing up, I worried there would be a war and they would be drawn into it. Now they are older and there is no draft so I don't worry as much—about them. Now I worry about my grandson and the duty that might fall on him someday.

Wouldn't it be great to have a period of absolute peace! I don't see that ever happening but it would be ideal. Maybe that's what heaven is all about.

So today I celebrate our independence. At the same time I celebrate I also pray for our leaders as well as the leaders of the countries with which we are not on good terms. The state of the world is a tenuous one and only a higher power seems to have the power to keep things safe. I pray and I hope, and I hope and I pray.

God bless America, and God bless the world!

## *Stop and Smell the Roses*

Is it me or does bad news come in waves for everyone? It seems lately all I have been hearing is bad news. It started when I learned a high school friend of mine's husband had died. I hadn't seen my friend lately and didn't even know her husband was sick.

Since the funeral was in another state I decided to call her. When she answered the phone, I was immediately taken back to high school when we used to talk all the time. Georgia was one of my best friends back then and we even had a radio show together our tenth through twelfth grade years.

I also remembered clearly that when my mother died, Georgia came to the house and sat beside me throughout the visitation. She made sure the responsibility for conversation didn't fall on me. I never forgot her kindness and I reminded her of it when I called to try and console her.

We talked for over an hour and it was not just about sad things. We talked about all our mutual friends and what they are doing. Georgia has always been a fountain of knowledge about all things happening in Clinton, South Carolina. We said our good-byes and ended on an upbeat note. Still it pained me to think of the sad times ahead of her as the reality of her loss sinks in.

A few days later, I learned another friend of mine has been diagnosed with cancer and it is terminal. This all came about quickly and sent me into shock. Once again I was reminded of how quickly our lives can change. One moment we are fine and the next we are facing eternity.

Over the years of my marriage, I have always told my wife and children that something isn't a problem if it can be fixed with money. Recently I forgot that. We had an air-conditioning unit break down. Replacing it was costly. Then the other unit acted up and we had to have the fan on it replaced, another costly expenditure. Then we had a leak in the upstairs bathroom and water came through the ceiling. The deductible was costly. And finally we replaced the garbage disposal.

I kept going around saying, "What next?" I said that until I got the message about these two friends and what they were going through. Then I shut up. These things can be fixed with money; they are not a problem. I had forgotten my own mantra.

I also had forgotten "It's not what you earn but what you learn. It's not what you spend but where you end." Those words are so true. We should strive to learn to be better and better people; we should live our lives so that at the end we know where we will spend eternity.

And finally we should all remember to stop and smell the roses, or as Tim McGraw sings "Live like we are dying."

## *When Is a Vacation Not a Vacation?*

I just got back from a visit to North Carolina. My wife and I went to visit our son JJ and his wife of one year Angela. This was really the first time we had visited them as a couple. Oh, we had gone to see them when they had only been married a couple of weeks but that didn't count. This was our first real visit.

We went to Durham on Thursday of last week and came back on Monday. That meant we were with them for three whole days and two partial days. Now that's a long time for me to stay away from home but honestly the time flew by. I think that's because we didn't have much planned to do. We just did what we wanted to do—and a lot of that involved eating.

Angela says she wasn't much of a cook before she and JJ got married. If that's the case, then everyone should watch those cooking shows. That's what she does and she has become an excellent cook. We had a roast dinner the night before we came back and it was out of this world. I mean I could have sat there and eaten for hours.

She and JJ had also gone out and gotten me tomato juice, cheese crackers with peanut butter, and peanut M&Ms. That was so sweet of them and made me feel really special coming into their home. I am big on the little things and this thoughtfulness really impressed me.

We also learned on the day we got there that Angela had been hired as a third-grade teacher for the fall at a private school in Durham—and they are so lucky to get her. Of course Angela is so lucky to have my wife Terry cheering her on. They spent every day talking about school and how to be the best possible teacher.

Then there was my "special event" while I was there. I was fortunate enough to arrange a lunch date with Jeffery Deaver. Jeff, as he likes to be called, is the author of numerous books including the new best seller *The Cold Moon*. I have been a fan of his for years and we had swapped e-mails for the past few months. I had met him at a function in Atlanta a few weeks ago but this was the first time I really got to know him.

He was off to Italy on a book tour the day after we had lunch so I was really appreciative he squeezed me in. I had a great time listening to him talk about creating Lincoln Rhyme and Amelia Sachs, the two main characters in his series of books.

I kept pinching myself as I heard him tell his stories. Am I lucky or what? A few weeks ago I had coffee with Deborah Roberts and her husband Al Roker, and now I was having lunch with Jeffery Deaver. Stick a fork in me, I'm done.

Back to the Durham trip. Another highlight of the visit was meeting Roxy, JJ and Angela's new dog. She is a year and a half old and just the sweetest dog ever. She is an inside dog and very well behaved. I really enjoyed her company while we were there.

The main joy of the trip was seeing how happy our son JJ is. He has really taken to married life and I am so happy for him. I guess all that praying we did about his wife for so many years has paid off.

Anyway I came away from our "vacation" feeling good about our trip. I am not a big vacation person but this one didn't seem too vacationy. It was just eating, relaxing, and having fun with my kids. I had a great time and I think they did too.

Now I am home and back into my routine which is also a good thing. I missed it. I honestly did.

## *True Caring Makes for Good Care*

My wife has had sinus trouble for years. Finally last week she decided to have something done about it: a surgical procedure to widen the opening into the sinus cavity. Sounds horrible to me, but she decided it was worth the time and effort to get it done.

As with most minor surgeries these days, this was to be an outpatient procedure. I had to have her at the ENT clinic by 12:30 and they would perform the surgery around 1:15. We arrived right on time (I am a stickler about punctuality.) and they started the paperwork almost immediately.

I was impressed from the start with how efficient and caring the people who were in charge of all this seemed to be. They didn't seem to be rushed about anything and they were helpful in getting all the information needed. They were constantly asking my wife if she needed anything or if she had any questions.

My wife is the type who needs to have everything explained to her in detail. If she has all the facts then she copes better. These people seemed to understand this and didn't seem to mind her questions.

Once the paperwork had been completed, my wife changed into a hospital gown. Then the nurses injected an IV drip into her wrist. My wife has small hands and finding a vein was not easy. The nurse kept apologizing with each prick. Again this was something she didn't have to do but it made me and my wife feel she was in good hands.

Before my wife went into surgery, the anesthesiologist came out and talked with us. He explained she would not be put to sleep but would be in a twilight state where she wouldn't care what happened. He also said she would not remember the surgery. Again he listened patiently to my wife's questions and answered each one.

While he was talking to us the doctor came in and explained what he would be doing. I never felt so thoroughly briefed on a procedure in my life. Each person involved was as informative and as caring as possible.

After they wheeled her out, I went in to the lobby to read a book and wait. In less than thirty minutes the doctor was back and was telling me how the procedure went. He was positive about everything and went into detail about each aspect of the surgery.

He took me back into the recovery room where my wife was. She was alert and talking with the nurses when I entered the room. She was a little out of it and was chattering away, which is unlike her. Still she looked great and seemed to be pain free. As she chatted she kept telling the nurses how nice they were and how much she appreciated their care and concern.

Amazingly by 3:00 we were on our way home. My wife had some antibiotics to take as well as some pain medication. For the next few days she took things easy but now seems to be just fine and her self again—without the sinus issues.

I know that medical techniques have made great strides, and that may account for how quickly she recovered from this surgery. I also believe, however, that it was the caring way she was treated by the staff at the clinic. A little tender loving care goes a long way and I think that's what really made the difference.

## Cell-O

A few days ago I called a friend of mine and he answered his phone "Cell-o." He was not saying the musical instrument but was answering in a word similar to "hello." When I asked if I heard right and that he had said cell-o, he responded I had called his cell phone. He stated he now answers his cell phone "cell-o" so people will know he is talking on his cell phone. That makes absolutely no sense to me. Who cares if he is answering his cell phone, his home phone, or his fax phone? I for one just want a simple hello.

This is an example of just how far our love affair with the cell phone has taken us. Now don't get me wrong. I love the fact I can talk to my sons every day, ten times a day if I want to. But sometimes I don't think the trade-off for that convenience is worth the irritation people and their cell phones cause.

For instance, I was at the bank the other day and the woman in front of me was on the phone with Bill. As a matter of fact she and Bill were having an argument. Seems he had driven her car and run out all the gas in it. (Did I really need to know this? No way!). When she got to the teller, she kept talking and passed her transaction over to her. Obviously something was wrong because the teller tried to ask her a question. But "Cell Woman" was so busy yapping she couldn't take time to answer the teller's question.

Another time, I was in a movie. Before the main feature started, there were big announcements asking people to turn off their cell phones. I complied. The movie was a drama that took intense focus to understand the plot. I was doing fine and really enjoying it until about ten minutes before the movie ended. A girl on the row in front of me flipped open her cell phone. It was like the beacon from a lighthouse had been unleashed.

I was furious and when she kept it flipped open I slammed the seat in front of me on her row. She turned around and gave me a look like I was insane. But she did close up her phone. Now what could have been so important that it couldn't have waited another ten minutes.

I keep hearing movie theaters are going to put in some kind of equipment that blocks signals for cell phones. All I can say to that is amen and hallelujah! I have heard cell phones go off in church, at weddings, and even at funerals. People have gone completely crazy when it comes to them.

You can't go to the grocery store without bumping into people who are having a great conversation. And it isn't just teenagers doing this. It is all ages and all sexes. We have become a society with cell phones pressed constantly to our ears.

So the next time you call someone's cell phone number, get ready for the response. It might just be someone who is so addicted to their private portable phone that they answer with a hearty "cell-o!"

## *Preparing for the Future*

My wife and I had lunch with some friends of ours recently. As we talked, the subject of preparing for the future came up. I was asked if I had cancer insurance—the answer is no. I was asked if I had assisted-living insurance—the answer is no. I have life insurance and I have health insurance but any additional coverage for an uncertain future, I do not have.

I wonder if I will need those types of extra coverages. But I don't wonder or worry enough to get them. I guess I still feel young enough that I can do all that tomorrow. Or the day after that. Okay, I know it will get here sooner than I think but I just can't worry about everything. There has to be some truth in letting tomorrow take care of itself.

More than the expenses, I worry about the toll it will take on my wife and children if they do have to take care of me during an extended illness. I know they will be loving and kind, or at least I hope they will. I do think that an extended illness is hard on a caregiver. It drains them and saps their strength.

Should I have to take care of my wife, I hope I would do it with love and strength. I hope that the heart of our love would give me the right mindset to be caring and compassionate. I hope that's how I would be, because in truth I can be short tempered and impatient. Also I do not like to be around sick people. Hospitals depress me to no end.

It all goes back to my mother's illness. Her death was a long one. When I reached a point where I thought she could not get better, and people told me she could not, I wished for it to be over. And I knew she wished it too. In the end she was in a hospital and it was a cold, morbid place where the lights seemed to always be low, and shadows surrounded everything. I hated it. I hated being there. I hated what it represented.

I don't dwell on this part of my life very often. I choose to think of the good times at every stage of my life. I think happy thoughts breed happiness and sad thoughts breed sadness. Maybe that's childlike reasoning but it works for me.

So I go on with my life thinking tomorrow is going to be as good as today and maybe even better. I am an optimist. I deal with the bad things as they occur but I don't wait for them to happen. And I certainly don't spend my time waging wars against possibilities.

Prepare for the future? Only on a limited basis. I cover the necessities but not the worst case scenarios. Call me a blissful fool but it has kept me happy for a long, long time and I hope it will continue to do so for many years to come.

## *The Critic as Actor*

For many years now, I have been supplementing my income by reviewing movies, plays, TV shows, videos, concerts, etc. I have praised people for their skills and criticized them for their lack thereof. I haven't set myself up as an expert but rather just write my opinions as I see them. In this respect everyone is a critic, I just happen to get paid for my opinion.

It has never been in me to be an actor. Oh, I did a play in high school my junior year, and then when I got to college I did a play my freshman year. I haven't done any acting since then and that was probably a wise move on my part. Knowing this, why have I now accepted the opportunity to be in a play at my church? My only response is insanity.

A few weeks ago, I was approached by a very nice man in our church who said they were starting a drama ministry. He said his wife was directing a play and wanted me to be in it but was afraid to ask me. I should have gone with that and let her stay scared but for some unknown reason I said she should call me. She did—and asked me to be in a play.

I told her how busy I was, but she said they would work rehearsals around me. I told her I was starting a book tour, but she said they would work around my schedule. She persisted, I resisted, but finally I gave in and said yes. I honestly never intended to say yes, but somehow I did.

We had our first meeting a few days later and the scripts were handed out. I took one look and thought, *This thing is long*. I was hoping for a fifteen-minute drama with maybe a cast of a thousand. This play runs for an hour and fifteen minutes and has a cast of six. And all of us have way too much dialogue.

Oh, yes, that's the other thing I meant to say. I can't memorize. At one time I could—when I was twenty. I ain't twenty anymore and my brain does not retain things like it used to do. I will never get all my lines learned. It did dawn on me that somewhere I read Marlon Brando had all his lines for "The Godfather" taped on the back of chairs, etc. During any scene that was being shot he just read them off the script. If it's good enough for Marlon it's good enough for me. I'll even send a Native American woman to pick up my award.

I do have a problem though that Marlon didn't. To my knowledge he never was a critic for any publication. I am sure he had his likes and dislikes but he never put them down in print. I have. So now you have the critic as actor. I would love to have the chance to review Roger Ebert or Joel Siegel in a play, and I am sure there are some people around here that will love the chance to see Jackie Cooper as actor. It might get brutal.

Still since I am doing a church play, maybe God will protect me. I am counting on that. That and a bunch of lines stuck on the furniture!

Now let's fast forward a few weeks. The play performances have come and gone. I was panicked up till and including my time on stage, but I do have to admit there were moments when I was in front of the audience and the lines were in my head that I was transformed into the character I was playing. Others may not have seen it but I felt it. Jackie Cooper shrank away to nothing and Joe Lumpkin (my character's name) emerged full force. When this happened I discovered the magic of acting and finally knew what makes people choose to do this.

Now don't panic. I am not going to suddenly abandon my family and head off to Hollywood or catch a plane for New York. I still have some sense in my head. Plus I know that even though I felt some sort of magic on stage, I didn't notice the rest of the cast of director being transfixed by my staggering debut.

*Memory's Mist*

Still it is nice to know that in a small way I have felt something of what the great actor have felt. I have known the rush of having my personality leave and a new persona come into my body. For brief periods I become the character I was playing and that was a thrill.

Now will I do other roles? I don't think so. I had a good time with this acting thing while on stage but I panicked about having the memorized lines leave me in the middle of the scene. Maybe if I had a photographic memory I would be lining up for another part. As I don't, I will make this my one and only stage appearance of my adult life.

I will still pursue my life as a critic but maybe I now have a little more respect for the actors who do this so magnificently over and over again.

## *Letters from Holland Street*

When I was growing up on Holland Street in Clinton, South Carolina, there were eight kids on my block. We were the offspring of three families. Keith and Mable Adair lived on the corner of the block with their two daughters June and Mary Keith. Next to them was the home of Grady and Virginia Adair. They had four daughters—Linda, Judy, Sue, and Trudy. Grady and Keith were first cousins, so those two families were related.

My family, which consisted of Tom and Virginia Cooper and their two sons Tommy and Jackie, lived two doors up the street in the house owned by Miss Bessie (Keith's mother). We rented rooms from Miss Bessie for several years and then moved down to the second block of Holland Street. Up until the time I graduated from high school, Holland Street was my home.

Linda, June, and Tommy were the older children. Mary Keith, Judy, and I were the younger set. Sue and Trudy were just babies. I describe us this way because this is the way Mary Keith captured us in her collection of letters *My Dearest Keith: Letters from Holland Street*.

The letters are those written by her mother to her father during World War II. Keith was in the Marines and served in various battles, but in particular he was on Iwo Jima during that fierce campaign. Mable wrote to him daily and as a diversion always told him what we children were up to. Mary Keith took the excerpts from the letters that described our adventures and made each of us Holland Street kids a bound collection of these memories.

You can't imagine how poignant it is to read about things my mother and father did with my brother and me and the rest of the neighborhood kids. I also enjoyed reading Mable's feelings about things. I remember her clearly even though she died in her middle thirties from cancer. She and Keith only had a few short years together after he came home from the war.

My best friend in the group was Judy. She and I were close since time began and are still close to this day. Strangely enough all eight of us stay in touch with each other. I guess the bond was tight enough to last a lifetime.

Grady and Virginia later had a son. His name was Ricky. Virginia and Grady divorced and Virginia and the children moved away. My father and mother remained on Holland Street and lived in our house until my mother's death. After she died my father married Grady's sister, Florence, and they built a new home next to our old house on Holland Street.

The deaths, divorce, and moves caused sadness on Holland Street. Still when you read Mary Keith's collection of letters, it is all sunshine and bright days. We eight kids lived an idyllic life during our early childhood. We all had three families and we moved interchangeably among the houses. There was always some place to eat, somebody to care about us, someone watching over us.

I wouldn't take anything for these excerpts of letters Mary Keith collected. They bring back a rush of memories that had stayed hidden in my mind. If you have access to letters, notes, anything that pertains to your past; collect them and get them in some sort of form to be handed down to your children. Believe me, the memories of this type are priceless.

The kids of Holland Street are a little scattered now but these memories keep us bound together in our hearts.

## *Expectation vs. Anticipation*

Last week we had the kickoff for my latest book *The Bookbinder*. A fairly large crowd attended and it was one of the outstanding days of my life. What made it extra special was the fact both my boys, their wives, and my grandchildren were there. My youngest son and his family only live a short distance from us (well, if you consider eighty miles short) so I thought they would come for it.

My older son and his wife live in Durham, North Carolina, so I definitely didn't expect them to be there. My wife, however, had arranged for them to fly in as a surprise to me. Do I not have the best wife possible?

My birthday is also this week so as an added treat my wife had arranged for all of us to go downtown and eat at one of my favorite restaurants. I was all excited about doing that and was taken completely by surprise when we walked into the area where we were dining and was surprised by ten of our closest friends. It was the perfect way to celebrate my birthday.

You have to understand the psyche of Jackie Cooper to see why this was so perfect. First off, I don't like holidays or special days of any kind and that includes birthdays. They depress me and I would just rather have a year full of ordinary days.

Second, when I know an event such as a birthday party is coming up I begin to build expectations about it. I plan it all out in my mind, and when it does not reach those expectations I get mad, sad, depressed, or all of those combined. I always do that. I build it up and expect it to happen—and as my good friend Susan Potts once told me, "Expectations will kill you!"

Now anticipation is a good thing. I anticipate things happening such as a radio show, a trip to Biloxi, or any event such as this. I relish the anticipation in the days leading up to the event. That's a

*Memory's Mist*

good thing. But if I ever tip over from anticipation into expectation, well, that's a killer.

Most of my problems with expectation come in the form of what I expect from my friends. If I had known I was having a birthday party, I would have wanted to know who was coming. Then if I found out someone had turned down an invitation for some reason I didn't consider to be valid, I would have been angry. Sorry, that's the way I am.

So for the birthday party to be a surprise was the perfect way to go. I didn't have time to ponder over it. As far as I know everybody who was invited came. There were no excuses given and so I didn't have to judge the value of the friendships.

I think maybe I am getting a little better as I get older (That birthday was a big one!). I honestly try not to expect too much from people. Still every now and then I do get disappointed and I can feel the righteous indignation building. My blood begins to boil.

Then that voice goes off in my head that says, "Anticipate, Jackie anticipate. Don't expect! Never expect!"

## *One Day at a Time*

Lately I fear I am becoming a recluse. Most days I prefer to stay in my house and read, watch TV, write, and wait for my wife to get home from work. I don't have a real need to go out and mix with people. I still do go out and mix and be sociable but my heart is not always in it. Most of the time I am thinking about how soon I can get back home.

It has not always been this way. In high school and college I always had to have a band of friends around me. And when my wife Terry and I were first married we were one of the most sociable couples you could know. When our children came along, we cut down on our social life but we still made time for friends.

Then after our children went away to college, we began to draw up the drawbridge a little bit more. We still went out to movies and to different restaurants but not with other people as much. We found we preferred each other's company over the company of others.

Just a couple of days ago I got a call from my friend Judy. Judy and I were part of the Holland Street kids that grew up in Clinton, South Carolina, so she and I have been friends for a long time. Judy told me her sister Sue's husband had been killed in a motorcycle accident. I couldn't believe it. It was one of those events that was just hard to take in.

Sue had also been a Holland Street kid, but she was a few years younger than Judy and me so we didn't hang around with her that much. Judy and Sue's parents divorced when we were around twelve years old and Judy, Sue, their sisters and brother moved to another town. Judy and I kept in touch, but I didn't see Sue that often.

As the years passed I would run into Sue in Clinton. After she got married I would see her and her husband at special occasions. This became more often after my father married Sue and Judy's aunt.

*Memory's Mist*

Eventually I met Sue's husband Rut. As my father always said, Rut was a good old boy. My father meant that in the most positive way possible as he said Rut was always in a good mood, always good to tell a story, and always looking out for people. I found all those things to be true too.

Sue and Rut always seemed like a couple who truly enjoyed each other. They had three daughters who they adore and now have been blessed with many grandchildren. On the Friday before his accident, Rut celebrated his birthday. All of his children and grandchildren were there with him for the occasion. I am sure that will be a real comfort to them in the future.

But what Rut's death brought home to me is that we aren't guaranteed tomorrow, or even the next minute. Life can change in a flash so if you have happiness, hold on to it and cherish it. Nobody lives forever and each day that passes is one day less we have with our loved ones. That may sound pretty fatalistic but it is true.

I love my life. I have for some time now. And I want it to stay the same. There is no one I enjoy like I do my wife and kids. So pardon me while I go out and polish the drawbridge. I am living my life one day at a time inside the castle of my home.

## *Biloxi—Blue, But Not Defeated*

Last week I made my first trip to Biloxi, Mississippi, in more than a year. I had always been a pretty regular visitor to the little Vegas on the coast, but then came Katrina and my sojourns to the land of video poker ended.

The reports I got from people I knew who lived there were horrific. Some of the big casinos had been virtually swept out to sea, and homes and offices were flattened and/or flooded. I wondered if this small town by the sea would ever be the same.

A month or so ago I got a notice from the Beau Rivage that they were opening back up for business, so a friend of mine and I made reservations to go for a few days. As we drove down the interstate outside of Biloxi, we didn't notice too much damage. And when we reached the Beau Rivage it looked the same. The stores on the inside of the hotel complex were not all opened, but it looked like they soon would be.

The next day after we arrived, we ventured down the street toward the east side of the strip. There we saw casinos that had just disappeared and were now a vacant lot. We also saw buildings that are just shells of what they once were. And the bridge that leads in from Ocean Springs to Biloxi is down. It was all depressing as could be.

Depressing, that is, until you talked to the people who were working in the restaurants, hotels, etc. These people have nothing but optimism. They told me that Biloxi is going to come back bigger and better than ever. To the person, they told me they planned to stay in Biloxi and raise their families there, and earn their livings there. There was no talk of abandoning this city and community.

Oh, I did hear some horror stories about the shelters where some people rode out the storm. One lady said it was hell on earth and that she and her husband and children only stayed one night. She talked of the peanut butter and jelly sandwiches they were served and the watered down red Kool-Aid they were given to drink. She talked about the bugs that were in the building and the unsanitary conditions.

Then she quickly added that was in the past and there is no sense in dwelling in it. There are happier days ahead, she said, and had such a smile on her face that she made a believer out of me.

That's what is special about Americans—their resilience. We get knocked down but we don't stay down. Biloxi may have the blues over what Katrina did but the city and the people are not defeated. Not by a long shot. It and they will come back stronger and finer than ever. I'd bet my favorite video poker machine on it!

## *Lonesome Town*

My wife and I have been married for over thirty years. During that time we have rarely been apart overnight. There have been some business trips here and there but nothing of a long duration. Well, I do remember one time when I was in the Air Force that I was away from home for three weeks. That separation almost killed us. The truth is we don't like being separated, at least I know I don't.

Currently my wife is in Florida. She has gone to visit her parents and my schedule was such that I couldn't go with her. She left on Sunday morning and she will be back on Wednesday. As I write this it is Tuesday—and I am miserable. The house just does not seem the same with her gone. It is too quiet, too empty, too spooky.

It's times like this I wish we had a pet. When we had a cat, it kept me company, good company, on those few occasions when Terry had to be away overnight. A cat is the perfect pet because it goes its own way and does its own thing, but checks in from time to time. But now we don't have a pet and you can hear a pin drop in this house.

My wife is a little over five feet tall and doesn't weigh much at all, still I feel safer when she is in the house with me. Last night I heard creaks and groans from every room in this house. I could have sworn I heard someone coming up the stairs. When it got quiet again, I came downstairs and rechecked the alarm system. Then I went back upstairs, closing and locking the door at the top of the stairs as well as the doors to our bedroom.

Sunday afternoon, I made my first run to the grocery store to stock up on all the comfort foods I could find. I bought tomato juice, cheese tidbits, fudge ripple cookies, potato chips and dip, and Diet Cokes. I plopped down in front of my TV and watched every show I had Tivoed this season but had not been able to watch. That included three hours of *Six Degrees* and three hours of *Brothers and Sisters*. Monday night I watched four hours of *Nip/Tuck*.

I have tried to get caught up on my reading but I just can't concentrate. I find myself reading the same page over and over. Writing is even worse. I start a paragraph and when I read it, it doesn't even make any sense. I have started a new book, so I need to get my mind in gear.

The truth is, to quote a song, "I've grown accustomed to her face." She truly does make my day begin. I know there are people who like separations in their marriage, and there are other couples who have to endure long periods of time apart because of their jobs. I just don't know how they do it. I like being married. I like being a couple. And when we are apart I am a miserable person.

Tomorrow morning she will leave St. Petersburg and head for home. We will talk constantly while she is on the road (thank God for cell phones), and I will be with her every mile of the way. When she gets back, I will put away the junk food. I will begin to read and write again. Life will return to normal and I will be a happy man.

But between now and then I am living in Lonesome Town, and I don't like it—not one bit.

## *Get Rid of the Blues with Jeans*

For me consistency is reassuring. In other words, I am a creature of habit. I love routine and hate change. In this mood and mode, I have lived my life. Nowhere has this been more evident than in the way I selected my clothes. I dressed nicely but samely (if samely is a word).

I think it was in college that I discovered khaki pants. There was a guy who lived down the hall from me and he wore khaki pants all the time. His name was Murk Bannister, full name John Murchison Bannister. He was distinct, and he was tweedy. He wore blazers with patches on the elbows, and he wore oxford cloth shirts. I had never seen anyone dress like this, and so I emulated him to some degree. In short I started wearing khaki pants.

Even after I was out of college I continued to wear khaki pants. I became fixated on them. When I entered the workforce I formulated a uniform of sorts. I wore a blue or white oxford cloth shirt, a striped tie, a blue blazer, brown loafers, and khaki pants. I wore this ensemble just about every day for thirty years. To say I was in a rut is like saying ice is cold.

My wife used to look in my side of the closet and just shake her head. There were pair after pair of khaki pants hanging side by side on the bottom level, and at the top was a collection of blue and white shirts. I always had at least two blue blazers to wear and two pair of brown loafers. Picking out my clothes for each day was not difficult in the least.

This formula for dressing continued up till a few weeks ago. It ended because my friend Dale Cramer (author of *Levi's Will*) and I were both invited to speak at an event. I showed up in my khaki-blazer ensemble. Dale showed up in blue blazer, white shirt, and jeans. He looked cool and comfortable. He also looked like a writer; I looked like a writer's uncle.

The next day I told my wife about what Dale had worn. She said it sounded nice. I had expected her to have a more forceful opinion. Still the next time I was invited to an event as a writer she suggested we get something new for me to wear.

At the mall, she suggested jeans. I immediately said no. I mean it was okay for Dale to wear them but Dale isn't paunchy like me. I could just imagine me blimplike in a pair of jeans—not a pretty picture. But my wife persisted and finally I gave in and tried on a pair of jeans. Just as I had imagined, I looked blimplike.

When I got home I put them aside and forgot about them—until it was time to get dressed for the event. Curiosity got the better of me and I pulled on a white shirt, stepped into the jeans, and added a blue blazer. Eureka, I had found a new me! I immediately felt younger, handsomer, slimmer, and more writer-ish. It was amazing.

Today I am living in the world of jeans. I wear them just about everywhere (okay, not to church), and I feel confident and happy. I have chased the blues away with jeans. I am out of my khaki rut and into the world of denim.

The moral here is that life can change no matter what your age. Call it a midlife crisis, or just call it getting out of a rut. My jeans have changed my life, and when I get that new red sports car my transformation will be complete. Just kidding!!

## Safe Alone

For most of my life, I have lived in a locked house, driven a locked car, and worried endlessly about the safety of my family. It's the way I am. I'm a worrier. When I worry, I worry most about random crime. I never worry I will be caught in a bad drug deal, or in the wrong part of town, or anything that takes an intentional act to be in harm's way. I worry about the random acts of violence that are not targeted at you but occur with you involved unintentionally.

Still I have to say I had a scare the other night. I had been in Atlanta for a book signing and was driving home. It wasn't late when I reached Macon, maybe ten at night. I looked down at my gas gauge and decided I needed to fill up. Also I saw a station that was advertising gas for $1.93 a gallon. That got my attention.

When I pulled up at the pump, there was no one around. I hopped out, put my credit card in the slot, and started pumping the gas. I was turned away from the road and didn't see anyone walk up behind me. But I did hear someone say, "Hey, I got a question."

I turned around and there was a young man standing a few feet away from me. He was fairly nicely dressed but he did look a little wild in the eyes. He then said, "I need a two dollar favor."

I don't know why that made me so mad but it did. And I gruffly said, "No way is that going to happen." I must have said it more forcibly than I thought because he backed up and said, "Stay cool, man."

He wandered off, or I thought he did. I finished pumping my gas and as I was getting in my car, another car drove up and stopped on the other side of the pump. Almost immediately this guy was back, and as soon as a young man (maybe twenty-one) stepped out of his car he asked for a two dollar favor. The young man gave him some

*Memory's Mist*

money, which was his business; but I did stay around long enough to make sure he didn't get accosted in any way.

It wasn't just the bumming money that bothered me, it was the fear this act caused. And I couldn't help but think this could have been my wife at this station and she could have been scared to death by this idiot asking for a handout. Maybe that's not charitable but that's the way I feel. I don't want my wife to have to fear for her safety any time she is out alone.

If you don't think bad things can happen, believe me they can. This past summer a friend's sister was murdered in Atlanta. She went bike riding on supposedly a very safe bike trail in Atlanta. While on the trail she was approached by someone who assaulted her and then kicked her to death. She was fifty-four, married, and the mother of three children. This shouldn't have happened. She should have been safe.

My friend has established a website www.safealone.org. You might want to visit it and read the story of her sister.

We should all be protected, we should all be safe, we should all be free from fear—but we aren't. Still things will never get better if we don't work to make them so. I know all panhandlers aren't murderers, and all people who ask directions on a bike trail aren't rapists, but some are. We have to learn to protect ourselves from the exceptions.

## *Give Me the Simple Life*

There are certainly people who enjoy living in Montana, Washington, and New Jersey, but for me the best place to live is in Georgia, specifically Middle Georgia. It is the place that best suits me and gives me a sense of enjoyment and awe every single day.

There is nothing like going to a big city every once in a while, but for overall living give me the small-town, simple life. In Middle Georgia I can actually still feel the sense of community and family I felt when I was growing up in South Carolina.

This past weekend just reinforced those feelings. On Saturday I attended the Georgia Literary Festival. It was held in Macon, Georgia, and it was an invitation for one and all to come celebrate the glory of books. There were guest speakers and panel discussions that featured authors from the area, but the main draw was the outdoor booths and sellers who sold books and promoted the literary legacy of this area.

The weather cooperated completely and it was bright and brisk all day long. I saw entire families strolling around, taking in the sights, and enjoying the sense of community that was offered. It was Americana pure and simple—and I loved it.

As soon as I finished with the festival, I had to race back to Perry for a booksigning at the Perry Bookstore. This was a part of a celebration of downtown Perry, and I didn't want to miss any of it. I also didn't want to miss my supper so I called my wife and asked where we were eating. She said she, my son, his wife, and their two children were headed to Cracker Barrel. I gave her my order for food and asked her to ask them to put a rush on it so I could eat and still get to the book signing on time.

When I got there about twenty minutes later, my food was waiting for me. Man, you can't get that kind of service anywhere else. In Perry even getting food is personal. I managed to eat my good food and then make it to the book signing on time. I mean I wasn't even late by a minute.

The celebration of downtown Perry brought out more families. My grandkids came down with their parents to enjoy the fun. One of the highlights was using colored chalk to draw pictures or sign their names on the main street—which had been blocked off from traffic.

One of the ladies who came to the signing that night runs a restaurant called the Swanson. I commented to her that the supper she had fixed for a church gathering that week had been delicious. It was a chicken and rice dish that was scrumptious.

When I finished bragging she told me she had some left over. "On your way home stop by and just tell Mark to give it to you," she said. She didn't have to say it twice. As soon as the booksigning was over I was out of there and headed to the restaurant.

The food I picked up was enough for three lunches for me, and I mean three big lunches. As I carried my food home, I reflected back on my day. It had been fantastic in every respect. And it had all been perfect for my kind of town in America.

I like to go to the big city. I like those bright lights and all the charms the big city offers. But when it comes to living you couldn't blast me out of Middle Georgia. In my book it is as close to perfection as an area can get.

## *Sweet Charity*

What is it with this direct approach of asking people for charity? I believe in giving to church and charities as much as anyone but I think it should be a personal matter, and not a response to a direct question. Lately the choice of giving or not giving has become an in-your-face issue.

At the grocery where my wife and I shop, you can not go through the checkout without being asked if you would like to make a contribution to a certain charity. Now I go back and forth to the grocery many times a day and I don't want to have to explain on each return trip that I already gave. I always manage to look and feel guilty even when I am telling the truth.

Also tonight I went to my local fast-food place to get a burger. As I was paying for it the guy behind the counter asked if I wanted to contribute to a certain charity. So now it is do you want to contribute, and oh by the way, do you want fries with that contribution?

If you do say no when asked about contributing, you feel like the scroogiest person ever. The clerks even look at you like, "Man, you are so cheap!" I want to defend myself, but isn't the whole idea of being charitable, keeping the whole thing private?

Then there are people who descend on your car in big cities like Atlanta, and wash your windows. I want to holler out the window that my windows are just fine, thank you. But have you ever tried saying something like that? You get such open hostility back!

I do think we owe something to those less fortunate than we are, and I have places I send my money, places I have investigated enough to think the money will actually reach those in need. I do not buy the random assertions that it is for the needy. I want to know specifically which needy we are talking about.

*Memory's Mist*

Today I got a call from a lady saying she was with the American Cancer Society/Red Cross/Leukemia Society or something like that. She said she would be sending me information about their campaign to get donations. I said fine. Then she said that she wanted to put me down for twenty dollars. I told her I would decide the amount of my gift when I got the paperwork in the mail. She then said something about she knew it would be at least twenty dollars. I repeated I would make up my mind when I got the paperwork. She closed by saying, "It is only twenty dollars, sir!"

Do I sound put upon? Well, that's how I have been feeling lately. I don't think giving should be the result of pressure. I think it should be from the heart and done privately. That's just the way I am, and that's the way I intend to stay.

## *Giving Thanks*

The holiday season is here already. I don't believe it! It was just summer and now it is Thanksgiving/Christmas/New Year's. We haven't even had but a touch of cold weather and the Christmas decorations are already up in my town of Perry.

The worst thing about all this is that there will be many days of holidays and that messes my week up. I love sameness and routine, and when the holidays come it means my paper won't be printed and my mail will be interrupted (thank God for e-mail that functions on holidays just as well as normal days). It also means I will eat too much, spend too much money, and blah blah blah blah blah…

The good thing is my wife loves holidays. She loves putting up the tree, decorating the house, buying the presents—all that stuff. My job is not to get too grumpy. Believe me that's a full-time job. Still I do make an effort; I honestly do.

And even if I don't like holidays I am grateful for tons of other things. Top of the list is my family. I am truly blessed in that area. I have the best wife in the world. She is beautiful inside and out, and has the most loving spirit of anyone I know. We have been married for over thirty years and I want a hundred more.

My sons are also special. I talk to them at least once a day and many days it is more than that. We all just like each other, as well as love each other. They definitely got the best of me and I am so proud of them I could burst. They are wise men too as they picked the perfect wives. I never had a daughter but I have two terrific daughters-in-law.

Then there are the grandkids. Uh oh, don't get me started. They are the most beautiful, the most loving, the smartest children you have ever seen. I never thought I could love anyone the way I love my children, but there is something really special about grandchildren.

I also include my brother in my family because in the past few years he and I have become really close again. We went through some rough years but now everything is fine. He and I talk at least every other day (God bless cell phones.) and we actually communicate. He is the last member left of my growing-up family and I cherish him.

Then there are my friends. Each and every person with whom I am close is special. I don't see them as often as I would like but when I do it is such fun just being around them. Friends are the icing on the cake of life.

I am more and more thankful for my health as I see and hear of people with terrible health problems. And I am thankful I can do work I enjoy and which gives richness to my life. There are hundreds of other things I could name for which I am thankful, but let me just say I am grateful for the little things in my life. These are the routine things, the common everyday things that make my life unbelievably good.

My life is great and I give thanks for it. I don't deserve my blessings but I surely do appreciate them.

## *My New Best Friend*

Author William Diehl died last week. He was eighty-one. He authored many books including *Sharkey's Machine*, *Primal Fear*, and *Eureka*. I read everything he wrote and I loved them all. There was something about the way Bill handled characters and plots that made me eagerly await each new piece of fiction he produced.

I first met Bill Diehl when he was living at St. Simon's Island. I had been asked to do a "personality profile" on him for *Georgia Journal Magazine*. I drove to St. Simon's to interview him at his house. From the moment he answered the door he and I were friends. I don't know what we had in common, but something was there that bonded us.

The whole time I was interviewing him, he kept saying he had made a new friend—and he had. I was in awe of him. In awe of his talent, his success, his love affair with his wife Virginia, and of his attitude toward life in general. He didn't just expect to have a happy and successful life, he demanded it.

I left St. Simon's that day thinking I had a new best friend. Bill said he would stay in touch with me and over the years he did. Now that doesn't mean we talked all the time. We didn't. But periodically I would get a call from him or an e-mail. He would have something intriguing to tell me and I would listen in awe.

One of the great things was that Bill never talked down to me. I mean, here he was a master of storytelling. I was an aspirer. He had more success than I could even imagine but he always celebrated my triumphs as if they were the equals of his. I was content to sit at his feet and learn but he lifted me up to his level with his friendship.

I never expected Bill to die. I knew he had had some health problems but I thought they were behind him. Maybe I didn't worry about his health because I didn't want to think of him as being sick.

*Memory's Mist*

Not seeing him very often made it easy for me to assume and pretend that he was just fine.

Bill wrote a blurb for one of my books. After he had sent it he told me that he was going to send me a generic blurb so I could use it on every book I wrote in the future. I told him that was a dangerous thing to do since I might write something he considered really awful. His response was "Not a chance!"

All those years ago when I first met Bill Diehl and he became my new best friend, I didn't have a clue as to how much I would miss him when he was gone. Now it has happened and I do miss him a lot.

Bill Diehl was a great writer, and I will hold on to his books forever. Bill was an even better friend, and I will hold on to his friendship even longer. There are a lot of people on this planet. Some make it a better place and some make it worse. The loss of Bill Diehl makes it a little less enjoyable than it was.

See ya, Bill.

## *Long-Lasting Love*

They are a couple who have been together a long time. I don't know exactly how long but I would guess they have been married for forty years or more. They have been married at least as long as I have known them and that has been over twenty years. Russell and Rachel are two people who look like they belong together. Don't ask me to explain that, it is just how they look to me.

When I first met them I noticed they complemented each other. He would say something silly and she would make it sound logical. Or she would say something pretentious and he would add to it and bring it down to earth. They were a perfect match, a perfect fit. I thought they were a sweet couple back then. I didn't give their relationship any more depth than that.

But then several years ago Russell got sick. He had liver cancer and took radiation and chemotherapy. Rachel was there beside him and took care of him in every way he needed. She told me one day she was going to love him into being healthy. And it worked. He seemed to have beaten it.

A few years later she began to have trouble with arthritis and then she fell and broke her hip. Things got complicated and it took her forever to mend. But whatever she needed Russell was there to provide. He was a constant cheerleader and nurse. And he did this even though he was aware his cancer had returned. I heard about it and asked if he had started treatments again. He replied that he hadn't, and then he added that he would start when Rachel got well.

Rachel is better now, though still a little shaky. And Russell has started treatments again. He is still up and about and has a positive attitude. And so does she.

I remember the first time I fell in love, or thought it was love. I was convinced there was nothing better than this way that I felt. It was perfect to be young and in love. It was the ultimate, or so I thought. But now I look at Russell and Rachel. They have been to hell and back and they are still in love. They are still tender with each other; they still complement each other; they still love each other.

Maybe I realize through them that sometimes love is wasted on the very young. Love at an early age can be transient, fickle, and not very long lasting. It is the love that has gone through the fire that's the most important. That's the kind of love we should all seek. I don't know if it happens that often but it is certainly the goal to which we should all aspire.

Life can be rough. Life can be treacherous. Life can be scary. But if we have a partner, a mate, a soul mate then all the things that life throws at us can be absorbed. That's the lesson Russell and Rachel have taught me. They taught me by living it in my presence.

## *R-E-S-P-E-C-T*

Recently I spoke to a couple of classes at a middle school. It was fun for me and I hope the students got something out of it, too. My talk was about serendipities or how good things sometimes just fall into your lap. We hear so much about the bad things these days that I wanted these kids to hear something optimistic and positive.

While I was at the school I noticed how strict the faculty is when it comes to keeping these kids in line. When I questioned it I was told that's how things are these days. If you show the slightest weakness then you are lost. So the teacher keeps solid control of his/her class and spontaneity and exuberance just aren't allowed.

This visit to the modern school system made me think back to my days in school. Now I know that was in another century and in a somewhat different world, but it wasn't that long ago. Still it might as well have been back in the Dark Ages.

When I went to school the teacher ruled the classroom, but she (most of my teachers were female) was a benevolent dictator. The main thing I remember about most of my teachers was how much they loved being teachers and how much they loved their classes. Now this was not a matter of a teacher actually coming out and saying that she loved us, but it was evident in the way we were treated.

And we loved our teachers. And what is more important, we respected our teachers. They got our respect because they were older than us, smarter than us, kinder than us. They taught by example in a lot of instances, and we admired them for who and what they were.

I think teachers today operate in an atmosphere of fear. Many are actually physically afraid of their students and in some instances that's well deserved. I also think teachers fear the administration because they feel their jobs are constantly on the line. It is strange that we hear how there is a shortage of teachers, yet teachers constantly fear they will be fired or their contracts will not be picked up for another year.

Fear can also manifest itself by teachers thinking their administrative staff will not back them up in a contest between the student and the teacher. When I was in school, the teacher was always presumed to be in the right. Now that's often not the case. I know I have heard parents of students talking and generally if there is a problem at school they wonder what the teacher is not doing that he/she should be doing. It is rare when it is presumed the student is not fulfilling his/her end of the bargain.

Respect needs to come back into the classroom. There needs to be respect for the teacher and the position he/she is in. The old presumption of "the teacher is right" should be re-instituted. A presumption does not mean a decision is absolute, but it puts the burden of proof on the student and I think in 99 percent of cases that's where it should be.

Surely there must be some way of getting the joy of learning back in schools, plus the joy of being a student. The school years should be days of enjoyment and learning. Somehow to me it all comes down to getting respect back in the academic halls. But maybe that's too simplistic.

## *Christmas*

It's beginning to look a lot like Christmas—*not!* At least not at my house. As I write this it is six days until Christmas and we haven't even put up a tree. There are no candles in our windows and no wreath on the door. People ride by and wonder if the Coopers are atheists, or just scrooges. I have begun telling people we are just supporting our neighbors who are Seventh Day Adventists. They have a decorationless home too.

The sad thing is we intend to decorate, but we just keep putting it off. In truth too my wife has had the flu and is just now feeling a little bit like her old self. All the boxes with decorations are in the middle of the living room and when she feels up to it we will start. That may be Christmas Eve but we will start.

I took a look in the boxes a few days ago and seriously thought about putting up some decorations myself. But then I knew my wife would just go behind me and redo. So I abandoned that idea. About fifteen years ago she was sick at Christmas so Sean, my youngest son, and I put up the tree. We haven't heard the end of it yet. We didn't put all the right decorations on the tree, we didn't put them in the right places, and we shattered some of her favorite decorations in the process. Three strikes and you are out!

I am not a big Christmas person, but I actually do miss the decorations this year. Well, I miss them the way my wife does them. They do look pretty when she gets them arranged and placed. Plus the kids and grandkids are coming and I want the house to look nice for them.

My mother always decorated for Christmas. I don't remember what the decorations looked like but I do remember the manger set we had. My brother and I would play with the donkeys and the cows and have them talking to each other. We left the shepherds and the wise men alone, and weren't allowed to play with Joseph, Mary, and the baby Jesus. That would have been a sacrilege.

After my mother died and my father remarried, my stepmother didn't decorate. She wasn't really into that. That should have been my first clue our relationship was going to be rocky. But after my mother died, I didn't care about Christmas for a long time so it really didn't matter whether we had decorations or not.

I am already fighting the Christmas blues. I can feel them descending around my shoulders. Hopefully having the grandkids here will keep me out of a total funk. For the last few years I have been civil at Christmas and not hiding in my room. My son Sean and I are both not exactly crazy about the season and we keep each other bucked up as best we can.

I even promised to take part in the church service last week and read the advent message. My wife Terry was supposed to light the candles before I read, but since she was sick with the flu a lady from the choir volunteered to do that duty. I could see people looking askance as they asked each other who that was with Jackie Cooper. I figure this is the year the divorce rumors start. And a ho ho ho to that!

I am sure by December 25 the house will have a Christmas glow. My wife is on an antibiotic and doing better. Once she gets started she is a dynamo. So bring on the season and let's get it going. And I promise to be as enthusiastic as I can be about it all.

## *It's Over*

Well, Christmas has come and gone one more time, and this time it was here and over before I knew it. I never got the Christmas spirit per se and I didn't have the Christmas blahs too much. One day it was an average day in December and the next day it was Christmas Eve.

I didn't want or need anything this Christmas so my wife and I decided to go to the beach immediately after the kids left and call that our Christmas gift to each other. The kids, I am sure, racked their brains and finally came up with my gifts that were two CDs by *American Idol* winners, and jeans/shirt/belt for my new phase of clothing. My granddaughter Genna gave me a Georgia Bulldogs visor while my grandson Walker gave me a "#1 Dad" coffee mug. The latter irked my granddaughter because, as she kept telling her brother, I am not his dad.

We spent Christmas Day eating brunch, opening presents, and then going to one of our closest friend's home for supper. Afterwards we came back home, watched a movie, and then went to bed. Pretty uneventful but satisfying.

I do have to say that it dawned on me after lunch on Christmas Day I had no one to call. We had called my wife's mother and let everyone talk with her, but I had no one to call. Now my father has been dead for over five years and my mother died when I was a teenager, so this was not a new thing this Christmas. Still it just seemed to hit me that I am now an orphan.

It is strange how you go along with your life not thinking about your status and then it hits you. Suddenly you are aware that there is no generation between you and death, no buffer so to speak. At this same time it usually hits you how fast time is passing. I remember taking my kids on trips with my father and stepmother, and now it is my wife and I taking our kids on trips with our grandchildren. We have become the older generation.

The new year looms ahead of us and I am looking forward to it. I have heard so many people say they hope that 2007 will be better than 2006. I don't know what was so bad about this year but it hit quite a few people wrong. I rather enjoyed the year. Maybe it is just that I enjoy my life so much these days.

I have survived the holidays with no visible scars and in just a few days I will be back to my normal routine. My youngest son Sean said to me on Christmas night, "It will soon be back to normal, Dad." He loves the everyday and I do too.

So for now it is off to the beach and then 2007. I look forward to it, I embrace it, I anticipate it. Life goes on, the days keep turning, and the blessings keep coming. Who could ask for more?

*Reflections from Route 2007*

## *I've Found My Face*

A few weeks ago a friend of mine's father died. When I went to his funeral I found myself being seated on the front row. It was at a church and all the family was on the right hand side of the church and the attendees were on the left side. I was on the front pew on the left side.

During the service my friend got up to say a few words about her father. I knew she would be eloquent and sincere, but I also knew it would be very hard on her, as she and her father were very close. Anyway when Deborah, my friend, got up to speak she started out by saying she wanted to speak on behalf of her brother and sisters. She added she did not know she would feel so emotional doing it.

She then segued into a story about Ed Bradley, the *60 Minutes* journalist who died recently. It seems Ed Bradley was asked one time to speak at a friend's funeral. He knew he was going to get emotional doing it so he asked another friend for some advice as to how to keep his composure. The friend told Ed that as soon as he got up to speak he should find the face of someone who would be supportive and encouraging.

Ed said he found the face when he was speaking and when he got emotional he looked at him, and "the face" in turn looked up at the ceiling. Then he found another face and he looked at him and that person looked out the window.

At this point Deborah said, "So don't move, Jackie Cooper. I have found my face."

Well, from that point on I was afraid to even twitch. I just wanted to stare straight at her and give her the support she needed. And something worked because she maintained her composure and gave a beautiful tribute to her father.

Later I thought about how honored I felt she had picked my face. It might have just been that I was sitting on the front row, but for whatever reason she did find my face.

Then I thought back on all the times I have just wanted to find the right face to give me encouragement. When I was little, it was usually my mother's face I sought out when I was performing in one way or another. I would look out in the audience and there she would be mouthing the words to a song I was singing or nodding her head in time to the music I was playing.

Once when my brother and I were visiting my aunt and uncle who lived in Charlotte, North Carolina, I got lost downtown. I was searching for my brother's face and when I saw it I thought it was the most wonderful face I had ever seen.

At one time or another we all need to "find the face" of the person who can get us through a bad time, or can give us encouragement in an uphill battle. Then there are the times when we need to "find the face" to share a really happy moment in our lives.

Our faces show our emotions. With a smile or a nod of our head we can be the encourager or whatever else we need to be. So keep a smile on your lips because you never know who is finding your face.

## *Talk Is Cheap*

Up until I was seven or eight years old I couldn't speak plainly. It was like I had my own language and the only person who could really understand me was my brother. My mother and father got some of the words and most of the intent, but only my brother knew my language. It was a very restrictive way to live. If I wanted to have a conversation it was with him or, well, no one.

Then for some unknown reason my speech and diction improved. I entered the world of clear speakers and with it came the freedom to talk with any and every one. I could communicate and it was wonderful. I wondered how I had ever lived without having actual conversations with the world. And I have been trying to make up for lost time talking ever since.

I love to talk. I really do. I could talk for hours, days, weeks, and years. I like listening to people and I think that makes for a good conversationalist. I like hearing what people are interested in, what they have done with their lives, what they hope to do in the future. I never tire of talking and I do a lot of it.

My wife is also a good conversationalist, but we talk in different ways. I talk in statements, which means I have a point usually to make and I get there. My wife talks in details. For example, if you ask me about a movie I give you the high points. If you ask my wife about a movie, she gives you the film from start to finish. It is a gift. When I miss a TV show and she has happened to see it, I just ask her about it and then sit back and listen. She can even quote dialogue.

When I go to visit friends, I like to sit around and talk. Lots of people have the TV going and talk over it. In my book, that's a no no. If I am going to watch TV, then I will watch TV. If I am going to talk, the TV doesn't need to be on. Plus I can watch TV at home. I can't have an extended conversation with my friends at home.

My wife and I have been married for a good number of years. I think one of the secrets of our success is we love to talk—to each other. We always have. From the earliest days of our marriage we have talked to each other about our jobs, our relatives, our dreams, and our kids. You name it, we talk about it.

They say that talk is cheap. Of course that's supposed to be a negative statement, emphasizing the importance of action. Still, I think of talk as positive. Talk is cheap; heck, it's absolutely free. Thank goodness for that. If I had to pay to talk, I would have been living in the poorhouse for many, many years now.

The important thing is that talk is communication. If we can communicate we can understand, and if we can understand we can make progress. Progress helps us to be better people and in turn makes for a better world. From two people sharing thoughts, to the world communicating that is a big step. But it all begins with two people knowing how and taking the time to talk to each other.

## *Foolish Fears*

Don't ask me why but I have always suffered from insecurities. For the most part, I have a healthy ego and know my strengths and my weaknesses. Still, when it comes to certain things, I am totally insecure. I fought against these feelings when I was a child and I fight them now.

These insecurities began when I was small and my parents would want to throw me a birthday party. I always said no. I wouldn't tell them why but I steadfastly said no. Eventually they gave up and just celebrated with the family around me.

What I didn't tell them was I was afraid no one would come. It was one of my worst fears. I would be there with my parents and no one would show up. I would die of embarrassment. Therefore I never had a birthday party while I was growing up.

When I got married and my wife and I had children, I went through misery every time either one of my sons had a party. Again I was panic stricken that no one would come. I tried to talk my wife out of having the parties but she wouldn't budge. I even told her why I didn't want my sons to have one. She said I was being silly and went ahead with the planning. And of course she was right. There was always a good attendance.

A month or so ago, I was talking with the head of the Sidney Lanier Cottage in Macon, Georgia. She told me about a program they had in which a poet or writer would come and read from their work. The evening was called a "Sidney's Salon" and she asked if I would participate in one. I agreed and we decided on a date in January.

A few days after I had talked with her, she called me and said she would need a list of who I wanted to invite. Panic hit me. This was like having a birthday party and no one showing up. If I was responsible for getting people to the "Sidney's Salon," I was in big trouble.

I explained my fears to my wife and once again she dismissed them. So I made a list and I gave it to the lady at the Sidney Lanier Cottage. Then I sat back to dread the night arriving. When the day came I kept telling myself it would all be over in three hours and I could stand anything for that long—even public humiliation. My wife cheerfully told me she didn't care if she was the only one there, I could read to her.

Well, to make a long story short the evening was wonderful. There was a good crowd of attendees and my stories seemed to be a hit. I ended the night on a real high, pumped up with the thrill of having such a warm and attentive audience.

On the way home, I thought back on how much fun I had had and then thought about what I would have missed if I had given in to my insecurities. I decided then and there that little fears were not going to rule my life any more. I had rather stick my neck out and try something that had the potential to be great than to miss it all together by being afraid of what might happen.

There are enough real things in life to worry us or make us afraid. We shouldn't waste our time on the little things. I am determined to put this new theory into practice. Heck, I might even have a birthday party next year.

## *Idol Chatter*

Last week I sat down to watch the first installments of this year's *American Idol*. My wife and I always enjoy these early shows when they show you the contestants with talent and without talent. The show is a mixture of the good, the bad, and the ugly. That's the way it has always been, and it's a successful formula that really pays off in ratings.

During the first two tryout shows, the panel of judges threw people out with a vengeance. In one situation, Judge Simon Cowell told a contestant he was a terrible singer and that he looked like a "bush baby." The guy took it with a grain of salt but the next day some in the media claimed that Cowell was too harsh or just plain mean.

I agree the "bush baby" phrase might have been a little too personal but the guy was a bad singer. I find it hard to believe that bad singers don't know they are bad singers, or at least someone near and dear to them ought to bite the bullet and tell them they are *bad*!

When I was in high school, we had a girl in our class who could not sing. I mean she was tone deaf. Still somehow her mother thought she could sing and was forever getting her to sing at special events or at church services. It was painful to hear and painful to watch. When she sang all of us kids would snicker or outright laugh and she would get upset.

I could never understand why someone didn't just tell her she stunk. To me that would have been kinder than letting her howl away and embarrass herself. When we graduated, she was still singing and may be till this day. Thankfully she is too old to audition for *American Idol*.

This girl was not alone in her no talent voice. I have been in many churches where someone will stand up in the choir and let lose with notes that could shred paper. These are not people who are just having a bad voice day. These are people who should only sing in the privacy of their homes. I know God loves a joyful noise, but even He probably wants it to be on key.

The whole point of *American Idol* is to find the best singer in America. It is not to encourage the non-talented. If a person is a shrieker or tone deaf they should be told. Anyone auditioning for *Idol* knows going in that the judges are going to be blunt, so it isn't like they are ambushed.

So maybe we should be just as honest with our friends about their talents. If someone can't sing maybe we can tactfully and gently tell them so. On the other hand maybe we had better not. We are not *American Idol* judges; we are just friends with an opinion. So maybe silence and earplugs are a better option.

## *My Country, 'Tis of Thee*

My brother called me this week to tell me he had gone to a swearing-in ceremony for a friend of his. His friend is from England and had applied to be a US citizen. It had taken a while but he had finally taken the test and now was going to be sworn in as a citizen. I knew this had been in the works but didn't think my brother was all that thrilled about sitting through such a ceremony.

When he called me he said he was glad he had been invited, as it was one of the most impressive events he had ever attended. It was held in Tampa, Florida, and a large number of people were sworn in. He said that one of the most exciting moments occurred when they read off the list of countries from which people had come to apply for citizenship. It was a long list and showed just how much of a melting pot America still is.

I could tell from his comments that my brother had been touched by this all, and while listening to him tell all about the ceremony I was impressed as well. I hope that someday I get a chance to view such a ceremony, and I think it would be good if we all did. Those of us who were born with American citizenship seem to take the whole thing for granted.

Plus I think that lately we hear only the negative about our country. The politicians and the news reporters seem to revel in their ability to tell us just what is wrong with America. Now don't get me wrong, I don't think our country is perfect but I do think it is pretty dadgum good. If not why would so many people want to come here legally or illegally?

I can remember when I used to get a lump in my throat whenever I heard the national anthem. I heard it a lot when I was a member of the Air Force and each and every time it made me feel proud to be an American. Now I only hear it at ballgames and don't have the same response I once did. It has become a song that delays the starting of the game. Most of the attending fans and the players just look bored and very few sing along.

Each day I get up and live my life taking for granted the safety I enjoy, the benefits that come from a free enterprise system, the security I have in attending my church. I am not persecuted for my values or my beliefs and I can vote or not vote for whomever I want. These are just everyday freedoms and rights that have become commonplace.

After 9/11 patriotism was at a high level. I can still remember how it felt in those days after the worst event in our nation's history. But time goes on and memories fade. We got back into our routines and the surge of patriotism subsided.

Maybe we all just need a makeup test in citizenship. Maybe we should have to renew it like a driver's license. Maybe then we would get back some of the respect for our privileged life in the land of the free. And maybe some of us would flunk. Think about that!

## *Voices from the Past*

A few mornings ago, I received an e-mail from my cousin Kem. It really took me by surprise as I haven't seen or heard from Kem in fifteen years or more. I instantly knew who she was but it took a moment for me to put a face with the name. In fact I had always thought she was a "Kim" instead of a "Kem."

Kem and her sister Mary Beth are the daughters of my first cousin Sue. Sue was always one of my favorite people and I had known her two little girls when they were growing up. They were a good bit younger than I was so I never knew them that well. Still with Clinton being so small you knew everybody in town and Kem and Mary Beth were always there at Cooper family get-togethers.

It was particularly interesting to hear that my father was Kem's favorite in the family. That doesn't surprise me. My father could charm anyone, and he did. She said he always called her "Kemtone" and when he would come into church he would always act like he was going to sit on her when he entered the "Cooper pew."

Kem and I also talked (by e-mail) about how large the Cooper clan was in Clinton, but they were never that close. My father had three brothers who were living in Clinton with their families when I was growing up but I can't remember being that comfortable with any of them. I saw them at church and we would have a "Cooper family" get together every now and then but it was not like a daily friendship of any sorts.

I think it went back to my grandfather, the patriarch. He was a remote man who kept himself isolated from his family. I never knew what he did for a living but secretly always thought his sons each gave him money to keep him going. He was always nicely dressed and he had a nice home—but what did he do? He was like one of those feudal lords of the manor. His sons and associates paid homage to him.

After he died I think the family kind of retreated into their own units. My Uncle Lynn and his family were the wealthiest segment of the family. He owned a car dealership and always seemed to have money and property. My Uncle Charlie ran a garage. He and his family did pretty good too. They had a big stone house on Main Street that always impressed me. It was Kem's grandparents' house and she told me she always found it spooky.

My Uncle Russell worked for my Uncle Charlie at the garage. He and his wife never had any children and both had some health problems. He was the uncle who always handed out chewing gum at church. All the kids would run to him before they went inside and he either gave them chewing gum or a nickel.

Hearing from Kem dredged up a lot of memories. It was like the faces of all those forgotten relatives now suddenly popped up with a smile. The Coopers of Clinton are virtually gone now. Only members of Uncle Lynn's family remain. In my memories, they are still there but in reality death has taken most of them away.

Hearing from Kem was a surprise. She had gotten one of my books from her town library and found my e-mail address on the cover. She decided to reach out to me and I am so glad she did. Voices from the past take you back "home," if only for a little while.

## A Trip to ABAC

A few weeks ago I made a trip to Tifton, Georgia to speak at ABAC College. ABAC stands for Abraham Baldwin Agricultural College, and for all the time I have been living in Georgia I thought of it as a "farming" school. Sort of like Clemson in South Carolina where I grew up.

I really didn't know much at all about ABAC. I had passed by the sign for it as I sailed down Interstate 75 heading to Florida. And both my sons had gone down to work at the Agrirama as part of a day trip at the school they attended. The Agrirama is part of the school where they grow crops just like they did in the 1800s. The people there dress up and use equipment they used back in that era.

Anyway, I was speaking to a group of students, faculty, and community members and I always like to do that. When I arrived at ABAC I went to the library where my host for the day was waiting. He introduced me to two students who were there to take me on a tour of the campus. This young man and young woman were well versed in all things ABAC. As they walked me from one place to another they spelled out the history and the future plans for ABAC.

One thing that impressed me was that each and every building, each and every improvement, cost in the millions. It was $3.2 million for this, $20.7 million for that, $1.8 million projected for those. Doesn't anybody do anything in the thousands anymore? I have a hard time wrapping my mind around millions. You can tell my mindset is still back at Erskine College in the sixties.

When I was in college we had two people to a room in the dorm, and it was just a room—a narrow room. We had a sink and a closet and room for two desks and a couple of beds. Students at ABAC can live in apartments on campus that have one person to a room with a shared bath in between. They also have a kitchen area and all of it is furnished. Utilities are included for less than $400 per month. Oh yes, they also have wireless Internet connection. Get out of here!

As I listened to these guys tell me about the food and the furnishings on campus I felt as if I had gone to college in a covered wagon, and fought the Indians along the way. Times sure have changed. And for the better in most ways. The campus at ABAC contains students of all races and creeds. And it certainly looked as if they all mixed together in friendly groups and were totally without discomfort. Now that's progress.

When the tour was over, I went back to the building where I was to speak. Speaking is something I enjoy and something that can go either really good or really bad. A lot for me depends on the audience. I feed on how they are acting and reacting. At ABAC on this day it was good. This group listened attentively, laughed in all the right spots, and later asked intelligent thought-provoking questions.

Before I left for the day I mentioned I had always thought of ABAC as just being a place for agricultural students, but that now there seemed to be a big mixture of majors and career fields. I was quickly told that though agriculture still is a vital part of ABAC, the main career fields for students are Nursing and Business. Agriculture comes third.

Live and learn, that's what it is all about. So if you are heading down I-75 and see the sign for ABAC turn off and take a tour. They are spending millions to make this an even better school for Georgia. It is apparently money well spent. At least to this outsider looking in.

## Book People Are Special People

For the past two weeks, I have been attending Book Festivals. The first was in Dahlonega, Georgia: the Dahlonega Literary Festival. This is its fourth year of operation. The second was the South Carolina Book Festival in Columbia, South Carolina, and this is its eleventh year. Both were well-planned venues that I enjoyed very much.

If you have never attended a book festival, you should. They are usually two days long and are chock full of panel discussions, author readings, and Q & A sessions. Delightfully, just about everything is free. Now how's that for a bargain?

In Dahlonega, the headliners were Diana Galbadon, Mary Kay Andrews, and Cassandra King. I have never read Galbadon or Andrews, but their novels are extremely popular. People were flocking to see and hear them. I have read Cassandra King's novels and am a big fan of hers. The fact she's married to my literary idol Pat Conroy also endears her to me.

I was on a panel moderated by Teresa Weaver, book critic for the *Atlanta Journal*. This was my first time to meet Teresa and it was quite a pleasure. She stated that she receives hundreds of books every week for review and only has room to review a small number each week. It is frustrating work but she perseveres. Plus a mention from Teresa in the paper can mean big exposure for a struggling writer.

When she introduced me, she called me a "writer's writer." I told her I could live on that remark for years. We writers take our compliments anywhere we can find them and hearing that remark from her was like discovering gold.

Brian J. Corrigan is the man behind the Dahlonega Festival and he really knows what it takes to keep book visitors happy. I have to add that the entire community of Dahlonega gets into the spirit of things and makes every author and every visitor feel right at home and very, very welcome.

In Columbia, Paula Watkins is the lady behind the scenes. I met Paula three year ago before she became the head of this book festival and I knew she was going to do great things—and she has. She has this festival down to a fine art. For the authors, well, each one is treated like royalty. From the minute you arrive to the exact moment you depart you are tended to with energy and expertise.

I love the South Carolina Book Festival. Maybe it is because I was born and raised in South Carolina and going there is like going home one more time. Each time I go there is always someone from my hometown of Clinton, or someone who went to school with me at Erskine, who shows up and speaks to me after a panel or a book signing. I have been going there for three years and it hasn't failed to happen yet.

The highlight of the South Carolina Book Festival this year was a panel I moderated on "Christian Writing in a Contemporary World." I had suggested this panel to Paula after my attendance at last year's festival. During the year we discussed it by e-mail and by phone. Finally we put together the "dream team" of authors that included Charles Martin, Beth Webb Hart, and W. Dale Cramer. I know these people personally and they are great Christian writers.

Towards the end we added Patti Callahan Henry and I knew this was going to be something really special and it was. On the morning, we got the panel together every seat was filled, people were lined up around the walls, and some were sitting on the floor. It was amazing. Plus Beth, Patti, Charles, and Dale were at their best. They spoke earnestly and intelligently. Then we took questions from the audience and it got even better.

I came home from Dahlonega and Columbia thinking about how special book people are, and by book people I mean those who write the books and those who read the books. I have always been treated with respect and warmth by those who talk to me about my writings, and I am treated as an equal by authors who are certainly more established than I am.

The book world is a great place to visit and festivals like these are the place to do it. Look up a book festival near you and go for the joy of meeting book people of all kinds.

## *Durham*

Last weekend my wife and I made a trip to Durham, North Carolina, to visit our son JJ and our daughter-in-law Angela. The other reason for our trip was for me to speak to a variety of classes at the Cresset School where Angela teaches. She had set up a schedule that would have killed a lesser man, but hardy soul that I am she and I knew I could handle it.

We left for Durham around 3:30 on Thursday afternoon. It was raining, and it continued to rain the entire length of our trip. At one point the announcer on the radio said something like "as long as you can hear my voice you are in an area where there is a tornado watch until two in the morning." All I could think of was that I sure would be happy when I could no longer hear his voice.

The trip to Durham took forever. I tried to drive cautiously but I also wanted to drive with some speed. My wife thinks fifty-five is speeding when it is raining. I kept praying she would go to sleep, but she kept waking up and saying, "Slow this car down!" It was a nightmare and it seemed to last forever.

We did get into Durham around one in the morning, and it was close to two when we got to bed. In the blink of an eye it was six o'clock and we had to get up and get breakfast, then head for Angela's school. Bleary-eyed but intent on being interesting, I pasted a smile on my face and faced the day.

The first class I spoke to was Angela's third-grade class. Each and every one of her students was adorable and I soon got caught up in their enthusiasm as I described my writing process and how all four of my books came to be. These children listened to every word and asked very intelligent questions.

One of the little girls in the class was named Imane. In my book *Halfway Home*, I wrote a story about a three-year-old girl I met on a flight to Los Angeles named Emani. The two names were close enough and the class listened spellbound as I read them the story of my meeting with Emani.

Later in the day I was talking with another class and there was an Imane in that group too. Once again I read "her story" to a rapt audience. Prior to meeting Emani on the plane trip I had never known anyone with that name. Now in Durham I met two children with a similar name to hers. It must be becoming a popular name, and it is beautiful.

All day as I was introduced to the different classes I would have the students tell me their names. God was surely with me as I seemed to have this amazing ability of total recall and could call each one by his/her name even later in the day when I would see them in the halls of the school.

Cresset was a great experience for me. I talked with kids in grades ranging from first to eleventh, and in each group; I found the students to be interesting and interested. I was tired when the school day ended at three that afternoon but it was a good kind of tired.

A few days later, I was back home in Perry, Georgia. The day we drove home the sun was shining and the traffic was light. It was a good day, and a good way to end a good trip. I have talked to my kids since we got back and they say the Cresset talks were a success. I hope so. Maybe there is a future author in their ranks, and maybe I helped spur his or her career along.

## *Missing Persons*

A few days ago I was talking with my brother and he told me he had contacted his old college alma mater and asked the whereabouts of three of his friends from those days. They sent him the address for one, another they had no address for, and the third had died last year. Well, I guess one out of three isn't bad. Anyway it got me thinking about some of my college friends and if I would like to locate them now. I only came up with one that I would really like to locate. All the rest of my college crowd, I know where they are.

When I started my freshman year at Erskine College one of the first people I met upon my arrival was Murch Alexander. He was from Greenwood, South Carolina, and he was like an alien from another planet as far as I was concerned. That's because he was "preppy" (Do they still use that term?).

Murch looked to me like someone from New England. He wore Oxford cloth shirts, khaki pants, blue over-the-calf socks, and saddle Oxford shoes. He wore his hair cropped close to his head, and on some days he smoked a pipe. He reeked of refinement and old money.

I had come to Erskine from Clinton, South Carolina, where we wore mostly jeans, madras shirts, and no socks. We thought we were pretty cool but we didn't stand a chance against someone like Murch. We acted our roles in life while his just came naturally.

Once I met him, I wanted to be friends with him, and we did become friends. I also started saving up for some Oxford cloth shirts. Murch was the kind of person who drifted through that first year of college without breaking a sweat. He got good grades and he made a lot of friends. After our first month, he was elected class president and I was elected vice president. Some of his charisma had obviously rubbed off on me.

All during that year, Murch talked about going to the University of South Carolina. That's the school he had originally wanted to attend, but his folks had wanted him to come to Erskine for one year. He did his duty and served his time, and after that one year he was gone. I never saw him again.

After Murch left there was a void. There was no one else who had his unique personality; no one else who shared my aspirations as he did. He was Kennedy-esque in his goals to change the world. If he could do it then maybe I could too. But with his leaving my save the world dreams became more realistic and I just settled for getting my degree.

During the years since I graduated from Erskine, I have looked at the newspapers in South Carolina to see if I could find some news of him. I figured he would have to be a state senator or at least a representative by now. But no luck. He is nowhere to be found.

So if anyone out there reading this knows the whereabouts of Hugh Murchison Alexander, once from Greenwood, South Carolina, let me know. I would truly like to know what happened to him and how his life has been. He is the one person from my college days that I would like to find. He was only in my class for that one freshman year but he made an impression.

## *What Is Celebrity?*

Because I write for newspapers and have TV and radio shows, I get to meet a variety of celebrities. I get to meet some who are on their way up, and I get to meet some who are on their way down. I meet some who take themselves very seriously and others who don't seem to have a clue that they are stars. It varies from person to person.

Several years ago Britney Spears made her first movie, a film titled *Crossroads*. I flew to New Orleans to interview her. When we met she was as sweet as could be, a little shy, but totally a professional. I had about ten minutes with her and during this time she never let down her guard. She was Britney and she conducted herself like she was playing a role. I wondered if she was ever just herself and somehow I doubted that she was.

The other extreme was Julia Roberts. I have interviewed Julia three or four times and each time I interviewed her she was having a great time. She was herself and let the chips fall where they may. I never had the feeling her answers were rehearsed or anything other than spontaneous. Plus she always let loose with that rich, throaty laugh of hers.

Julia Roberts is probably one of the most famous actresses in the world today but being around her you would never know it. She doesn't act like she thinks she is something special. She is just herself, and believe me that's enough.

Mel Gibson impressed me as someone who didn't enjoy the celebrity part of celebrity. When I interviewed him, he seemed ready for the whole thing to be over. I didn't think he had any personal animosity towards me, he just didn't like the whole celebrity process.

The same was true with Hugh Grant. I have interviewed him several times and every time I talk with him he states how he doesn't think acting is a very serious profession for a man. He always says he is thinking about quitting and starting a career as an author or something more formidable.

One of the most down-to-earth people I have ever met is Ice Cube. He treats his career as a business and he is totally savvy about what it takes to make it go. He knows the entertainment side, the business side, and the public-relations side. Of all the celebrities I have met, he is the one who seems to have the best clue as to what it takes to succeed.

Then there is John Travolta. John is the friendliest celebrity I have ever met. He always seems happy to see you and always calls you by name. John is not your guy next door. He is John Travolta. John is aware of his celebrity but he enjoys it. That's the impression I get from him. He enjoys being John Travolta and he wants you to enjoy it too.

Celebrity is a funny thing. It enhances some lives and destroys others. Some people are aware of how famous they are while others act like they are just ordinary people. And in truth they are all just human beings like the rest of us. They are just richer and better known.

## *Bless the Beasts and the Children*

Last weekend was the Cherry Blossom Festival/Mulberry Street Arts and Crafts Show in Macon, Georgia. For the past five or six years my fellow author Jackie White and I have had a booth at this event. We sell copies of our books and have a great time. This year we both had a new book to sell. She had a mystery titled *Mockingbird in the Moonlight* and I had a collection of short stories titled *The Bookbinder*.

Last year the weather was awful. It rained so hard that Sunday's events were cancelled. Usually the arts and crafts festival is held on both Saturday and Sunday. The year before that I had almost frozen to death. You never know what the weather is going to be like in Middle Georgia in March.

This year the weather was predicted to be clear and hot—and it was. The temperature climbed up into the mid-eighties on Saturday and to near ninety on Sunday. Luckily we have a tent that keeps us out of the sun. It did get a little warm but nothing like it was out in the open.

My friend Jackie White is an animal lover. Every year she would observe the pets strolling down the street in front of our tent and comment about how hot and thirsty they looked. This year she decided to do something about it. She brought a metal bowl and some containers of water when she brought her books. She also had a sign that read, "Dog Refreshment Center."

The water and the sign were a big success. People were amazed that we had refreshments for their pets. And, boy, did those dogs lap it up. We had dogs of all sizes stopping by for a drink. One dog was as big as a Shetland pony, and another was one of those tiny nervous dogs that looked like he could be stepped on and destroyed.

*Memory's Mist*

As happy as I was about the dog refreshment idea, I wish we had also had baby bonnets to hand out. I saw way too many babies in strollers with nothing covering their heads. I hope their parents had slathered them with sunscreen but I don't think so. As the day progressed, I saw little people getting pinker and pinker.

What really confused me was that most people brought their pets and babies out in the middle of the day. The festival went from ten in the morning to six at night but the big crowds were out around the noon hour—the hottest part of the day. In the late afternoon as the weather got cooler, the crowds got smaller.

I have a feeling there were a lot of babies having a hard time sleeping Saturday and Sunday nights because they were sunburned. Maybe not. I hope not.

Next year when we are preparing our tent and other paraphernalia for the festival maybe we will remember to bring the bowl back along with the water. And maybe we will have a "Bonnet for Baby" sign put up too. Or maybe the festival planners can come up with a cheaply made baby cap that will have the Cherry Blossom logo on it.

Better yet let's add the logo of "Bless the beasts and the children." That says it all.

## *Making a Mountain out of a Big Hill*

Anybody who knows me knows I am not much of a tourist. I don't have any yens to see the Seven Wonders of the World, or to travel around the world in eighty days. I prefer to stay at home, and when I do travel I prefer to do it by car even though that limits my circle of sightseeing.

When I accepted an invitation to take part in the Lake County Festival of Reading, I did so knowing I could get there by car. Being in the middle of the state of Florida, it wouldn't even be that much of a trip. So a few weeks ago I got up early and started my trek to Mount Dora, Florida, where I would be spending the night. I was going to speak at the library in Paisley, Florida but Mount Dora would be my home base.

I took the interstate down to Wildwood, Florida, and then switched to the parkway that goes to Miami. Armed with directions I had gotten from Mapquest (God love 'em), I made my way slowly to Mount Dora. I got to the town, but couldn't find Heron Cay Bed and Breakfast where I would be staying. A quick call to Randy and Margie, the owners/managers, and I was off again.

When I found the B&B I was overwhelmed. It looked like a Victorian-era home sitting across from a lake. It was one of the most beautiful settings I had ever seen. And inside the house there were more surprises. It was all furnished with the utmost care and taste. My room had two queen-size beds and comfortable plush chairs everywhere. I felt like a king.

Margie and Randy showed me around the downstairs and told me all about breakfast and when it would be served. They also offered directions to some of the best restaurants in the area. I didn't get a chance to talk with them for long as I had to get changed before my host for the evening picked me up.

The next day I awoke rested and ready for more sights. I ate breakfast at the B&B and then packed up for my drive to Clermont where I was speaking that afternoon. Randy told me I would be going by one of Florida's rare mountains. It was called Sugar Loaf or Sugar Hill or something like that. He said it was a real mountain, or at least a great big hill, and that it was definitely worth getting off the main road to see. I decided against doing that. Getting lost is always a danger for me so I stuck to the road I knew.

Clermont was another pretty city by a lake. No wonder they call this place Lake County. There were lakes everywhere. I felt like I had been taken out of Florida and dropped off in New England. This area just didn't look like the Florida I knew.

After I got home I began to brag on the towns and communities I had seen. I was surprised at how many people did know of the area, especially Mount Dora. My mother-in-law told me she had actually gone on a tour to the area and found Mount Dora to be sweet and quaint.

I am still not convinced I want to be a world traveler, but I do want to go back to this area of middle Florida. My wife would love it all. Plus I want to see that mountain I missed or at least that big hill.

## *The Joy of Living*

Last week my son and daughter-in-law let us have the grandkids for a few days. It had been a while since they actually stayed with us without their parents being present. To celebrate this event I asked them what they wanted to do. Their answer was—go bowling!

Genna is now seven and Walker turned five on Saturday so they can actually get into the bowling thing. My wife begged off because she has had some back trouble in the past, so it was left up to me to be the adult who bowled with them. It has been some time (years actually) since I bowled so I was pretty rusty.

For the kids they now put up bumpers so they won't gutter the ball. I was hoping they would just leave them up for me too, but no luck. And I have to admit a few of my throws ended up in the gutters. Still I didn't throw the ball backwards (which I have done in the past), and I didn't throw it into another lane (which I have done in the past).

We bowled two games and Genna came in second in one game, and Walker came in second in the other game. It couldn't have worked out better if I had planned it. Plus I am only mildly sore from my exertions.

The next day being Walker's birthday, he went to an Atlanta Braves game with his parents and other grandparents. We gave him some money to spend at the game and when he returned he had spent it all on a cap for Genna. He dearly loves her. Genna meanwhile had gone shopping with my wife and had gotten tons of clothes. She loves to shop and she loves to buy.

The next day was Easter Sunday and we all went to church. It felt so good to have most of my family with me. My oldest son JJ and his wife usually come home for Easter but this year his wife's parents had come to visit them so they stayed in Durham.

After church we went out to the home of two of our best friends. Other couples and their families were there too and we had a real Easter celebration. I love being with my friends on holidays. I am not a big holiday person and this helps me forget to be depressed. We ate a lot, talked a lot, and enjoyed each other a lot. It was simple but it was wonderful.

The children had an Easter egg hunt and Genna found the golden egg. The prize inside was twenty-five dollars. I should have joined in the hunt. She was a little too boastful about finding the egg but Walker seemed to tolerate her success.

It was a good day, a joyful day. It was nothing complex, nothing that cost a lot of money. Time passes and life seems to get ultra modern at times, but it is the old enjoyment of faith, family and friends that always gets me through. I enjoy my life. I love my life. And weekends like the one that just passed make memories for me to treasure for years to come.

There is joy to be found in the simple things. There is joy to be found in living.

*Someone to Watch over Me*

As I write this, the Virginia Tech massacre is only a day in the past. It is the most horrible tragedy of this type that has ever happened on American soil. It is heartbreaking and gut-wrenching in its horror and the thoughts of so many deaths is enough to depress us all. And as the dust settles, everyone is asking "why" and "how" and there are not many answers yet.

One issue did stand out in my mind and that's the fact that the members of one class were lined up and shot execution style. That means one man with one gun held twenty-five to thirty people at bay and shot them individually. How could that happen? Why didn't they charge him and take away the weapon? Did they just stay there in line and wait to be shot?

Now I am not saying I would have acted any differently; none of us can say how we would have responded to that threat. But when did we change from a society who would protect itself to a society that waits for someone to protect us? We have got to go from reactive to proactive if we are going to survive in this world as it now exists.

This is the same mentality I perceived when I saw the film from Louisiana after Katrina. I saw people waiting for someone to come in and do something for them. But it didn't happen very fast and people were left on rooftops and in huge stadiums. People held on to their belief that the government was going to come in and help them and it didn't—at least not quickly enough.

At some point, whether on a rooftop in a flood or against a wall awaiting execution from some deranged killer, we must say, "I am mad as hell and I am not going to take it anymore." And, yes, that's a quote from Peter Finch's character in the film *Network*. There's a lot of truth in his rant, as we cannot always play the victim card. Twenty-five people could have taken the Virginia Tech killer since he only had one gun and it was not an automatic weapon.

For too long we have been living in our cocoons and have had someone else worry about taking care of us. Now the world has changed. There is evil out there and it is determined to beat us down. We have to take care of ourselves and take care of our families, and when someone says they are going to harm us we have to stop them from doing it.

This is not a cry for vigilantism but rather a call to take care of yourself. As Christians we are taught to turn the other cheek but when it is a you-or-them situation I say go with righteous action. It is a sin what happened at Virginia Tech. I look at the faces of those who were gunned down and I cry for them.

I think of the people who were on United Flight 93 that crashed in Pennsylvania on 9/11. They stood up and fought back. True none of them survived but they weren't going to survive anyway. In this instance at Virginia Tech maybe if they had acted as a group some of them would have survived.

Of course this is all speculation but it does have some probability in being true. Depending on big brother or whoever to take care of us may not be the best way to go any more.

## *Online Dancing*

A friend of mine told me the other day that he was signing up for an online dating service. I was appalled and told him this has to be the dumbest things to do ever and he replied that everybody was doing it. Based on his assertion, I asked some other friends of mine if they knew anyone signing up for online dating services and they said they did. Obviously it is the new way to meet people, especially for the younger generation.

Still I think it's creepy. I mean you can swear to be twenty-five years old, movie-star handsome, and many other good things—online. Yuck! Still maybe in this day and age it is the quickest and the safest way to go. You can correspond with someone a while before you actually meet them, and maybe these dating services do conduct some kind of screening.

I have never participated in an online dating service. They didn't even have such a thing when I was dating. We just sent a message by a dinosaur and waited for an answer. I have participated in certain writers' groups online and I have to admit after you have e-mailed, blogged, or whatever with strangers for a while they actually become your friends.

One group I participate in has a woman in the group named Annie. She is a writer under the name of Luanne Jones and has had several books published (*The Southern Comforts* and *Heathen Girls*). She always writes interesting posts on this group site and I had commented back and forth to her about different things. This was our only communication and I didn't know what she looked like but she did know me from my website.

Anyway this past weekend I went to Bowling Green, Kentucky, for the Southern Kentucky Book Festival. This is an event where you are in a huge hall with slews of other authors and you meet people and sign books. This goes on from ten in the morning until three in the afternoon.

Around noon a woman walked up to my table and said hello. Then she added, "You don't know who I am, do you?"

My response was, "I'm sorry but I don't. Should I?"

She then held up a copy of *The Southern Comforts* and said, "That's me."

I jumped up from my chair and raced around the table to give her a hug. I was so glad to meet her. She was just as warm and personable in person as she had seemed to be online. We talked for several minutes and I even got to meet her husband and son. It was a real reunion.

Now when I "chat" online with Annie I will know who she is and what she looks like. And I guess that's the way it happens for those people who set up dates online. However, I would be much more eager to find a friend online than to try to find a mate.

Still the electronic age is here and communication has taken on a whole new meaning. You have to move with the times or be left behind in a cloud of dust.

## *Simply Southern*

Recently I was on a radio show in Atlanta, Georgia, that took phone calls from the listeners. This is always a seat-of-your-pants situation for me because you never know what you are going to be asked. I was on the show to promote my book *The Bookbinder* and I was hoping the questions would be about stories in my book.

What I got were numerous questions on being Southern. One of the questions I was asked was about Southern traditions; in particular what did I think of three Southern heritages: going to church as a family, having meals together and sharing a lot of food and talk, and celebrating the family as a unit.

My family always went to church together when I was growing up. We were Baptists so that meant Sunday morning and Sunday evening services, and there was prayer meeting on Wednesday nights. We sat on the Cooper pew and I always felt secure there. I was baptized in the church; I sang in the church children's choir, and when I started dating I took my dates to church.

My Uncle Charlie and Aunt Maynette always had the best dinners for the family. Aunt Nette loved to cook and she could turn out some big spreads. The Cooper clan usually gathered at their home at least once every couple of months and it was something to look forward to in advance. The best thing she made was country-style steak with mashed potatoes. I loved it. I could eat my weight in it and I think I tried to do that every time we got together—of course that was back when I could eat anything and everything and never gain a pound. Those were the days! My family gets together with friends these days and has "bring a dish" meals together and those take me back to the days in Clinton, South Carolina, when I and my family sat down at Aunt Nette's table.

*Memory's Mist*

As for celebrating the family, I am afraid I celebrate only my immediate family. My brother lives in St. Petersburg, Florida, and my parents are both dead so it is basically just me and my wife, our sons, and their families. I have not kept up with cousins and I used to do that. Days pass and we drift away from the family circle. Maybe one of these days we will have a Cooper family reunion. It would be fun.

Another caller asked if I thought a "Southern way of life" would still exist in fifty years. I answered that I certainly did because "Southerness" is based on the climate, the culture, and the people. That combination makes us Southern and we assimilate people as quickly as they can move South.

There is a Southern pride that makes us unwilling to adapt or adopt any other way of life. We treasure our slower ways, and cling to the values we have always had. That doesn't mean we don't progress—we just do it in a Southern way.

The variety of questions I got about being Southern indicated to me a need for people to feel we are holding on to our roots. They seemed to want to be assured that our way of life will be with us for years and years to come. I think it will; I hope it will. To me being Southern is simply the best way to live. It is the way I have always lived and hope to continue.

So if you want to join the Southern way of life then come on down. We will have the churches, the food, and the families waiting. Y'all come.

## *Hello Outdoors*

People who know me know I am not an outdoors person. And by that I mean I rarely go outdoors. Now that doesn't mean I am a recluse. I just go from my house to my car to wherever I am going and it is rarely any place outside. That's why seasons don't bother me. I am always warm in the winter and cool in the summer thanks to heaters and air conditioning.

But today I spent some time outdoors. I went to tape a radio show and the people I was supposed to meet had not gotten to the studio when I got there. The door was locked and I was forced to wait outside. That's when I noticed what a gorgeous day it was. I hadn't seen a day that pretty in years. The temperature was warm and there was a breeze. It was a perfect day.

Sitting outside I began to think back to my childhood. When I was a child, I spent most of my time outside, especially during the summer. I would leave the house early and stay outside all day long. We had a forest behind my house and all of us kids would play down there from dawn till dusk. We built a fort, a treehouse, and every other adventuresome thing we could contemplate.

We were all tanned brown as berries and never ever wore shoes. Most of the boys just wore khaki shorts and that was it. We were all great friends in my neighborhood and we would moan and groan whenever a rainy day would force us inside. But you know in my memory there were rarely any rainy days in my summers. And when it would rain it wouldn't last long and then we would go out and play with our boats in the gulleys that ran in front of our houses.

There was a big field up from my house that had tall grass in it and we would play soldier there. We would sneak through the grass and shoot or capture each other. At other times we would mash the grass flat and use it as a means to spy on cars coming down our street.

*Memory's Mist*

We would religiously write down tag numbers and if a car came down our street too many times we were sure it was someone spying on our neighborhood.

Our imaginations were boundless in those days and adventure seemed to be around every corner. There was always someone to play with and always some game to play. It was a happy neighborhood and a close one.

I don't know when I decided I didn't like the outdoors. It was probably high school. That's when I became a little more complex and things weren't as bright and sunny. I was unhappy with my father's new wife and I spent a lot of time in my room, hiding away from her.

Today when I spent my moments in the sun I made a pledge to see the sun more often. I think I can take the heat in small measures. Plus I live in a beautiful area of the country and it is a shame not to enjoy it.

Of course as I sit here writing this I feel a sneeze coming on. And another one. I do have some allergies, and now my eyes are running. Maybe spending time in the outdoors wasn't so smart. Maybe I will just look out the windows every now and then and be satisfied with my indoor life.

## *A Gift from God*

My wife's father is very sick. He lives in St. Petersburg, Florida, and is in the veterans' hospital. My wife spent all last week there with him. He was alert and aware of everything and they had a great visit. Today she got a call that he had taken a turn for the worse so tomorrow morning she will fly to St. Pete again.

I reminded her today of what a great visit she had with her father last week. She had told me how much they reminisced and how much they had laughed. I told her I thought that was God's gift to her.

Terry's dad being sick brought back memories of my father's last days. Daddy had always been a big, robust man. He always got a lot of exercise and looked healthy. Then toward the end of his life, my stepmother became concerned about his weight. He was diabetic and she worried about what kind of food he ate. As a result he got smaller and smaller, thinner and thinner.

I think people look healthier when they have some weight on them and Daddy's loss of weight worried me. But I was not his caregiver, my stepmother was. She was always telling me that Daddy didn't really have an appetite any more, but when we took them out to eat he ate everything on his plate.

The last time I saw him, we had gone to Clinton for a visit. His memory had become spotty but on this day he knew me and Terry both. He asked about our sons, JJ and Sean, and also about our grandchild. He was pretty much with it all afternoon. When we got ready to leave I kissed him on his head and told him I loved him. He told me he loved me too.

My stepmother Florence walked us out to our car but while we were standing there talking Daddy came to the back door. Florence went up the back steps to see what he wanted. When she came back down she said, "He just wanted ya'll to know he loves you."

That was the last time I saw him alive. He died the next week. Someone asked me later if I had a chance to say goodbye. In a way I did. I had those few hours with him and I think they were a gift from God. It was one of the closest times we had had for a long time. I always felt my stepmother stood between my father and me. From the time, they married there was a line between me and them.

But on that last day, the line was crossed. Somehow Daddy and I connected. Maybe he knew the end was near and he reached out to me one last time. Or maybe God just wiped that line away for us.

I think Terry had a wonderful visit with her father last week. Whether or not he will know her this week is an unknown. He is very sick and is basically drugged up and sleeping. Still I hope she knows she can always remember that last visit she had and the great communication between them. It was her gift from God. At least that's what I think.

## *Like a Hole in the Head*

A year or so ago I hit my forehead on my car's trunk. I was reaching in to get something and whacked myself good. A bump came up on my forehead and stayed there. It didn't go away and didn't get smaller. Finally when I had my yearly physical my doctor told me I should have it checked.

I went to Dr. Clark Kent and he biopsied the bump. It came back as a basal cell cancer, which is the simplest form of cancer to cure. I clung to that thought. He set me up an appointment to have it removed via a process called "Mohling." I thought he said mowing and I could just see them mowing down my bump like a weed on a lawn.

When I showed up to be mowed, Dr. Kent said they were going to take out a plug in the shape of a pie tin. He said they didn't care what was in the middle of the pie. They were just concerned about what was on the sides and the bottom. He said they would make the cut and then test the tissues. I was to wait in the waiting room while they tested it all.

The mowing didn't hurt at all, and soon I was awaiting the results. In about forty-five minutes to an hour the nurse came out and said all was clear. That was a great relief. Now all I had to do was get it sewn up. But before they started sewing, Dr. Kent handed me a mirror and told me to look at what they cut out. Like a fool, I did as he said. That's when I almost lost my breakfast. I mean, they had taken a chunk out of my forehead.

Now they had to squeeze the incision together and sew it up from the inside out—sixteen stitches. All I could think of was when James Earl Jones told me I looked like Peter Boyle. Peter Boyle played Frankenstein's monster in the comedy "Young Frankenstein."

Madeline Kahn always called him her little zipper head. Well, now I truly did look like Boyle as a zipperhead.

The doctor gave me a prescription for the pain. Macho me didn't think I would need it. And I really didn't the first day. But when the numbness started to wear off, I was begging for that prescription. Luckily, the medication made me sleepy so I slept through the pain.

I get the stitches out in a few days. Meanwhile I have a bandage on my head that makes me look like I am a World War II casualty. I have gotten quite a lot of stares and more than my share of attention. The attention is nice.

Hopefully, this is the last time I will have to have something like this done. I am going to try to watch out where I am going and not hit my poor damaged head any more. You know that old saying, "I need that like I need a hole in my head." Well, I now have that hole in my head, and I don't need anything else!

## *A Trip to Memory*

A few days ago I went to Clinton, South Carolina, which is the place where I was born and raised. I don't go back there very often since my father and mother are both dead. I still have a few relatives there, but no one I am especially close to. The purpose of my visit was to get some furniture out of the house my father and stepmother shared. My stepmother is in a nursing home now and will not ever return to her home.

The furniture I was picking up belonged to my mother. It was Kershaw furniture and I wanted it to be in my home and eventually passed on to my children. I also wanted some family pictures that would mean something to me and no one else.

My father and stepmother's home is right next to the house where my mother and father lived along with my brother and me. Going into the house of my childhood was the event that evoked the most memories. It had been twenty or thirty years since I had been in it and the memories came back with a rush.

It was the kitchen that made me the most nostalgic. I looked at it and suddenly I could remember cold winter days when we would rush from our bedroom to the kitchen to stand in front of the oven. Mother would make us cheese toast and we would have coffee milk to drink.

It was in the kitchen where our dogs always had their puppies. Mother would bring our dog in when her due date was near, and she would keep her inside until the puppies were born. We were kept out of the kitchen during the birthing process so when we got to see our dog she would be lying there with her puppies around her.

The kitchen had a back door that led into a fenced in backyard. I remember being a child and thinking the steps that led down into the back yard were so high. They don't look high any more. Also the backyard was huge in my childhood memories and now it's like a

*Memory's Mist*

postage stamp. How in the world did we ever ride our bikes back there? There is hardly enough room to turn around.

As I peered into the bedroom I shared with my brother in my mind, I could see all the furniture that used to be there. Our beds were lined up in an L-shape against the corner where the windows were. We slept with the windows open and there was always a breeze blowing into the room. No wonder I slept so good growing up.

Standing in that house I could close my eyes and hear the squeaky voices my brother and I used to have. I could hear the low murmur of a tune my mother used to hum. I could smell the bittersweet sweat of my father when he came home after a long day's work. It was all there waiting to be remembered.

The house I grew up in is the house I lived in when my mother got sick and died. Even with that traumatic event occurring there, it is still a house with good memories—unlike the house next door where I have mostly bad ones.

I don't know when or if I will ever go back to Clinton. The past is gone and the memories that were good I carry with me. Still I am glad I made that last trip home. It was good to visit the past one last time.

## *The Greatest Generation*

My father-in-law died last week. He was eighty-four years old but I still had hoped he had several more years left on this earth. His name was Joe Millard and he was an exemplary individual. He was also a member of what Tom Brokaw has called "The Greatest Generation," those people who were born prior to and during the depression and fought the good fight during World War II.

Joe was a member of the Navy and saw duty during WWII. Although he was born Scottish and was not a citizen when he enlisted, he argued with the recruiter that we were all fighting the same enemy. He and his brother Danny were accepted for duty in the Navy and Joe became a citizen after the war ended. Danny did not make it home from the war.

Joe adored his brother Danny. Just days before Danny was killed, Joe learned that the ship he was on and the ship Danny was on would cross paths in the Pacific. Somehow they arranged to be on deck at the right time so they could wave to each other. It was the last time Joe saw Danny.

When Danny entered the Navy, he left behind a girlfriend named Mary Lou Matson. Everyone knew they would be married when the war was over. When Danny didn't return, Joe and Mary Lou consoled each other and that consolation turned to love. They married and had been wed for sixty-one years when he died.

Family was everything to Joe. He wanted his kids to grow up and get married but he would have been happy if they had all lived next door to him. Out of the four children, three remain in the St. Petersburg, Florida area. My wife was the only one who moved away.

I remember clearly that after our honeymoon in North Carolina my wife and I went to St. Petersburg to pack up our wedding gifts. When it came time for us to leave, I didn't think Joe was going to be able to handle it. Terry, my wife, was the first child to get married and it was killing him that she was moving to Georgia.

When I was trying to get Terry into the car, Joe was holding on to one arm and I was pulling on the other. Eventually he let go but he wasn't happy about it. Later she told me that when he was walking her down the aisle at the wedding he whispered in her ear, "You can still call this whole thing off."

Joe's love for his wife and children never wavered. He was a prime example of a devoted husband and father. At his funeral, his children spoke glowingly of how great he was to them all. And an abundant number of friends also praised him to the family.

Joe's generation worked hard, loved hard, and lived life to the fullest. He was devoted to his God, his country, and his family. He will certainly be missed by all who loved him. As his generation dies out we will be left with a void in America.

## A Week at the Beach

As I write this I am sitting on a balcony on the third floor of a condominium in Panama City, Florida. The sun is shining brightly and the ocean is sliding up on the beach. The water is as blue as I have ever seen it and the people at the beach and around the pool are in danger of getting burned. Up on the balcony, I am safely escaping the sun but am enjoying the ocean breeze.

Me being at the beach is a miracle, or something like that. I do not like vacations and getting me to the beach for seven days—well, it took an act of congress or the threat of my wife's eternal anger. Plus our good friends, the Borahs, own this condo and they generously offered it to us for the week. My son, daughter-in-law, and two grandkids also decided they wanted to come. My older son and his wife couldn't make it, but they were invited.

I am having a good time, but I miss my routine life in Perry. This morning I went out looking for a *USA Today* and thought I would never find one. I came back and worked the crossword puzzle and proved my mind is still working. I have already read one book since we arrived and have three more I want to finish. I have plenty of reading time as the rest of the family loves the beach and pool.

Yesterday afternoon I took everyone to the movie. There is a new theater near here called the Grand. I bought several large cokes and large popcorns for the group. When I asked if these included free refills (like they do in Georgia), I was told no. The girl selling the goods said I could send a complaint to their website if I was unhappy. A simple I'm sorry would have sufficed.

There is a large crowd of people here in Panama City this week. I have talked to people from Illinois, Tennessee, and Rhode Island. Everyone appears to be in a good mood and all appear to have money to burn. I am always amazed by how affluent vacationers seem to be.

*Memory's Mist*

Tomorrow night we are all going to gather around the TV set as my son is doing "color commentary" for an All Star Game for the Southeastern Independent Baseball League. He is excited about doing it and we are all excited about seeing him on TV. If anyone knows everything there is to know about baseball, it is my son JJ. He has never wanted to do television before but does seem excited about this opportunity.

JJ is the managing editor of *Baseball America* and has used his baseball knowledge in his job there. Now he can relate some of the inside stories he knows in order to make the baseball game on television more interesting. Who knows, this could lead to a full-time job on the air.

A movie here and there, some good books to read, the cool ocean breeze blowing, and lots of good food to eat—this week might be pretty enjoyable after all. But, believe me, this time next week I will be back in Perry, Georgia, happy as a clam. I will be following my routine and living my life to the fullest.

A week at the beach is a lot of days, but maybe I need a little variety in my life from time to time—as long as it doesn't happen too often.

## *The Time Is Right, I Mean Ripe*

Last night my friend the farmer called. He told me he would be coming by my house this morning at 6:30 and leaving a package on my back steps. I asked him if he meant the time was right. He said yes, the time is ripe.

I hardly slept at all thinking about what the morning would bring. And sure enough as soon as I awoke I headed for my back door. There on my steps was a bag containing fresh, wonderful, luscious...tomatoes! The time was ripe indeed.

You can't imagine how excited I get about tomato season. This year I thought it would never get here. We had a late freeze in Georgia and it messed everything up. I kept asking my farmer friend for a progress report and he kept telling me to be patient. He said tomatoes have a mind of their own. The days crept by and summer started and no tomatoes. But today here they are.

I have always loved tomatoes. Since my childhood in South Carolina I have salivated whenever I thought of a sweet, fresh summer tomato. Oh, I eat tomatoes year round but that means I have to suffer through the plastic kind you find in grocery stores. What an insult to your palate they are, but if you can't get the real thing you take the next best thing.

I love tomatoes with eggs for breakfast, tomato sandwiches for lunch, and tomatoes with steak or whatever for the evening meal. There is no food that can't be made better and more enjoyable by having a red tomato on the side.

I also love tomato juice, drink it by the gallon. I think tomato juice and Cheez-its or cheese-and-peanut-butter crackers is the perfect breakfast. I don't however like V-8. Those people who say, "Oh, I could have had a V-8!" aren't true tomato lovers.

*Memory's Mist*

Maybe there is something nostalgic about my love of tomatoes. My father always had two or three tomato plants in the backyard and we would get a bumper crop just about every year. Plus our neighbor Henry always had more tomatoes than he could eat and brought some over to us. My mother, father, and brother liked them but nobody loved them the way I did, and do.

Recently, I have discovered how great tomatoes are for your health. There are vitamins and other things in them that are very beneficial. Doesn't that just make sense? They are nature's way of giving you good food and good health.

So now you know why I was so excited to get the call that told me the time is right and the time is ripe. The next few months will be bliss. I hope they are for you too. Remember all it takes is for tomato season to arrive. Happy eating!

## *You Are What You Car*

Today, I bought a new car. Just like that. It didn't take a lot of research or days of trying one car out and then another. I just went to my local Saturn dealer and bought it. I didn't get a sports car (My midlife crises is on hold.), or an SUV. I didn't look at red cars or convertibles. I just went with a standard sedan in silver.

As I looked at the car, it brought back something I heard years ago. My best friend Tucker told me, "You are what you car." In other words, if you wanted to be seen as slightly edgy, pick a slightly edgy car. Or if you wanted to be sporty, pick a sporty car. I looked at my silver sedan and repeated to myself—you are what you car. And I car conservatively.

Now inside my new car I have OnStar and Sirius Radio. I also have leather seats and radial wheel covers. So what you see is not completely what you are getting. The same with me. I have my moments of adventure.

Cars though have never been a big thing with me. I just want something that gets good mileage and is reliable. That's why I traded cars. My wife's car (She gets my hand-me-downs.) has been acting up. I really didn't feel safe with her driving it back and forth to school every day. Plus it has 169,000 miles on it. We do tend to drive our cars till they drop.

I honestly tried to get my wife to take the new car, and I am going to keep on her about it. But she says she only drives to school and so she doesn't need the newer car. However she has been oohing and ahing over Mini-Coopers. She thinks they are cute. I even heard her telling a friend that she thought the convertibles were great. If I hear her saying, it would be nice to have one in yellow or red I will know her midlife crises has kicked in!

*Memory's Mist*

One reason I keep cars for so long is that I become attached to them. A few days ago the car I have been driving wouldn't start. I came out of a movie theater and it just wouldn't catch. I called my wife to come get me and then I called a towing service. After I made these calls, I said I am going to give it one more try. The car started.

When I got it to the garage, they said it was a bad sensor. They also told me they couldn't believe the car started. But I understood. My car had reached down and summoned all its power to make the engine start one more time. That's the kind of relationship I have with my cars. They take care of me and I take care of them.

That's the kind of tender loving care I will give my new car. The one that says I am a silver Saturn sedan kind of person. I am what I car and I'm doggone proud of it.

## *My Mother the Car*

Years ago there was a TV show titled *My Mother the Car*. It concerned a young man whose dead mother had been reincarnated into a car. The car, of course, spoke to him and gave him advice constantly. The whole premise of a talking car was supposed to be so preposterous as to be hilarious.

A few years later *Night Rider* came along. It starred David Hasslehoff and concerned a man with a car possessed of superior intelligence. It talked too. Again this was supposed to be something that was way out of the ordinary, the stuff of futuristic stories.

Well, it didn't take long for the future to arrive. Today we have cars that talk to us. My new car is equipped with one of those systems where you can ask directions, where to eat, and a million other things. The first time I punched a button and a voice came on and said "Hello, Mr. Cooper, how can I help you?" I couldn't help smiling from ear to ear. It was really weird.

After I got the car, my wife and I drove down to Florida. The car dealership had put in a tank of gas for us and this car gets good mileage. We were in St. Petersburg, Florida, before we had to gas up again. When I hopped out to fill it up, I looked at the gas cap flap and it was flat against the car. I searched for a place to insert my fingers and open it up. Nothing.

I hollered for my wife to look up in the manual as to how the tank could be opened. She couldn't find a thing. I searched again for some way to open the gas cap flap on the side of the car. I had no luck. Finally in desperation I decided to call "the voice."

When I heard "How can I help you, Mr. Cooper?" I told her I had a stupid question. "There are no stupid questions," she trilled. Then she proceeded to help me. All I had to do was mash the middle of the flap and it would pop open. Who knew?

*Memory's Mist*

There are other fun things on my car. There is an info button you can press and see how hot it is outside. Or you can find out how many more miles you can go on the tank of gas. Plus you can see what kind of gas mileage you are getting or check as to how much oil has been burned. It's amazing. And I haven't even gotten to the Sirius radio yet.

The radio has 946 channels. Okay, I am kidding but it has a lot of them. They include sports, country, talk, jazz, Spanish, and kiddie stations. I found myself flipping between them all until my wife slapped my hand.

Cars don't actually drive themselves these days, but they are getting pretty close. It won't be long before we can just state where we want to go and the car will drive us there. How do I know? My car told me.

## *The Great Outdoors*

Last weekend my wife, my sister-in-law, and I went to Dafuskie Island, South Carolina. I had been invited to be part of a panel speaking before a group at a section of the island called Haig Point. I had eagerly accepted the invitation because the lady in charge of getting the panel together had long raved to me about Dafuskie Island. Her name is Patti Callahan Henry and she lives there part time in the summer.

The only way to get to Dafuskie is by ferry. You park your car at a welcome center for the island and then get on the boat. Patti told me my car would be totally and absolutely safe, but this was the new car I had just bought. I felt a little scared at leaving it alone and unattended, but I did.

The ferry voyage was fine, just a few bumps every now and then. It took a little over thirty minutes to reach the island. Once there, we checked into a place called the Mansion. This is an old home that was built years ago on St. Simon's Island. It was going to be torn down but some people got the idea of moving it to Dafuskie. They put this 7500-square-foot building on two barges and moved it lock, stock, and barrel to the island.

After we were shown to our rooms, we were told that if we wanted to explore the island, there were golf carts behind the Mansion with our names on them. This was a new experience for me. I had never driven a golf cart. Hey, I'm not a golfer.

Anyway, I first had to ask where the key was. It was on the key ring for my room. Then I had to ask how to start it. The guy in charge told me to turn it on and go. I asked again how to start it. I was expecting to hear some kind of motor starting.

The guy told me to put it in gear (To the right was reverse; to the left was forward.). I thought he meant you had to put it in gear to start it. I know this guy felt like braining me cause he finally came over, moved me over, and showed me how to drive the thing. Once I understood I liked the whole battery concept and we scooted around the island just fine.

The scenery was beautiful, and the homes on the island are awesome. I did keep an eye out for snakes and I almost choked when I saw signs that said, "Don't molest the alligators!" I thought "molest" was a rather strange choice of words.

Patti had told me there were tons of activities on the island. You could go crabbing, shrimping, tubing, boating, etc. I was fine with just carting.

My wife and sister-in-law went on and on about the beauty of the scenery, the symphony of sounds, the joy of getting back to nature. I kept looking for a Golden Corral. There is nothing like that there. There isn't even a movie theater.

I had a great time meeting the people on Dafuskie and the panel was a real joy. When we left the next day, I was raving about the fun I had with the people. My wife and sister-in-law had their heads together trying to figure out how we could all come back next year with my sister-in-law's husband included. They talked about wanting to stay for a couple of weeks.

A couple of weeks! No way! I would go berserk. The peace and quiet as well as the beauty of nature would not do it for me. My wife says I would de-stress. I say I would up my stress level. I like to see nature. I am glad nature is there. But to dwell among the beauty for two weeks would be like water torture for me.

Dafuskie Island is a great place to visit but I wouldn't want to vacation there for more than a weekend at a time. Too much communing with nature is the anti-vacation for me.

## *The Circle of Life*

Things seem to come in cycles; good times follow bad times and then back again. Right now I am in a good cycle. My spirits have been up and opportunities are coming my way. And when one opportunity comes, it seems two or three will follow.

I have also come to observe that success follows success. Take for instance the writing of books and getting them published. I never dreamed I would get one book published. Things like that just didn't happen to people like me. Then one day I got lucky and got a publisher.

When I finished my second book, I had an easier time finding a publisher, and by the third I was able to negotiate a better deal. I am now working in my fifth book and I have a publisher who publishes everything I offer. That may not always be the case but it is the way it is now.

My point in this is that once you have success in a field the later successes are easier to find. Just last week I was offered a source where my entertainment reviews will be printed. It is with a small newspaper but the money is good. On the same day I found out about the newspaper offer, I got offered a new radio show. On that one day, the hits just kept on coming.

So what makes certain times be full of good things? I honestly do not know. I don't know if it is the alignment of the stars or just random good luck. I know sometimes I can feel good things coming and it seems to be when I am in a good frame of mind. So maybe keeping a positive attitude is the key.

My good moods seem to come in cycles too. I don't understand that either. Most of the time I'm just on an even keel but some days I will have terrific highs. The world will seem brighter and more wonderful in every way. But then I will hit a patch of not so great times, and that's no fun at all.

Before I married I used to give in to my "depressions." I would sink and wallow in them. To tell the truth, I enjoyed them a lot. But then after I got married my wife said she couldn't put up with the ups and downs of my moods and I learned to hide the lower ones. It can be done. And as I hid them they became less intense, and now I don't have any feelings that are nearly as low as they once were. And that's a good thing.

Without these deep lows I have become a glass-half-full type of person. That has made my life happier. I feel compassion for anyone who has those real low points. That must be the deepest kind of despair. Maybe anyone who has that kind of low needs to work on suppressing the dark feelings. I am sure it wouldn't be a change overnight but it might help over the long haul.

Life is full of circles and cycles. I have found that to be true and I live with that belief. If today is dark then tomorrow might just bring the sun for a time of the greatest joy you have ever known. I hope so!

## *He's Flying the Plane*

Religion has always been a big part of my life. I was raised Baptist and my family went to church just about every time the doors opened. I was saved and baptized when I was twelve, but I didn't find true faith until I was fourteen. That's when my mother died; that's when I found God.

Over the years I have been better at religion sometimes and sometimes not, but my faith has never wavered. When I first went off to college, I remember thinking now I don't have to go to church. For a month or two I didn't. I just slept in on Sunday morning. Then I began to miss it, and after a while I really missed it. I like the way going to church makes you feel and I like the people I meet in church. So I started attending again. During that time I was neglectful of my religion, but I never lost my faith.

After I got married and had children, I was even more regular in my church attendance. I had now become Methodist and I really like our church. Plus I thought it was important that my children be raised in the church. You learn a lot of good lessons for life there.

Lately I have been thinking more and more about my faith. I don't talk about it a lot, but it is there. As a rule I don't debate politics and religion, so my friends and I don't have deep discussions about those subjects. I think a lot of people are like that.

A friend of mine asked me one time why I didn't talk about religion much. I didn't have a good answer. I guess it is because I don't have a strong fixation on religion. I see flaws in all the Christian branches. Still I have to have faith. It's what keeps me going.

God is the center of my faith. Having Him in charge of my life helps keep me sane. I also cling to the concept of an afterlife. If this is all there is, then what has been the point? Plus I want to be reunited with those who have died before me.

*Memory's Mist*

What got me to thinking about all this is a story my Sunday school teacher told this week (Yes, I do go to Sunday school even though that makes me sound like I am ten.). The story went like this. There was an airplane flight from Los Angeles to Atlanta. Halfway across the country the plane hit turbulence. The plane rocked and shook and swayed up and down. It seemed to go on forever.

All of the passengers were scared silly except for one little girl. She was about eight and she sat in her seat and colored in a coloring book while all this was going on. She never cried; she never asked anyone for reassurance; she just sat calmly throughout the turmoil. The man across the aisle from her was stunned by her composure.

When the storm was over and things had calmed down, the man asked the little girl why she hadn't been afraid during the ruckus that had been part of their trip. The little girl looked him in the eye and said, "My daddy is the pilot and he's flying this plane. He's taking us home."

That basically sums up my faith. It doesn't get any simpler than that.

## *Now Is the Time*

The other day I was eating lunch with some of my friends. There were five of us, all males in ages ranging from thirty-something to sixty-something. One of the men stated he sure wished he cold be college age again. Three others quickly chimed in that they wished that too. I was the only one who said he liked the present age best.

The others looked at me like I had been dropped on my head. They could not understand why I would not want the wonderful years of my youth to live over again. I said I would like to stay the way I am today for the next fifty years as long as my health remained the same, and the people I loved stayed around and their health remained the same. No way, my friends responded. They would all like to be younger. Not me.

When I was college age, I was constantly short of money. I worked part time when I was gong through school but that didn't give me enough. I was constantly trying to scrape together enough to date or to buy gas. It was hurry up and catch up and then get behind again. Today I have some extra money and I don't worry nearly as much as I used to do.

Plus college was when the cheerleader and I broke up. So I spent the next few years worrying when I would meet the right girl. Or worrying that I might never meet the right girl. At the present time, I have the right girl by my side and I am super happy. Why would I want to go back?

I think we reach a certain age of life when we start looking back too much. People I know who were miserable in high school and college now tell me they long for those days. Wake up! They weren't that great. Most of us didn't reach our capacity as far as personality, intelligence, and certainly maturity until we were well out of college.

In high school and college, I was intense. Everything seemed to be do or die. I stewed and fretted over too many things—things that proved to be unimportant or even nonexistent. Today I am much more laid back and don't take life or myself nearly as seriously as I did then. If I had had a graph of my emotions it would have been highs and lows, highs and lows.

One of the wisest things I remember my Daddy telling me was there were no good old days. He had lived through the Depression. These days we are living now are the good old days he said, and he was right. Oh, there are things I miss about the days gone by. It was a more innocent time in some ways, but every generation thinks that.

I like the day-to-day excitement in the world of today. A few years ago cell phones weren't common, computers were only for the rich, and the mail still came to your home or post office boxes and not through e-mail. I like these changes. I am technologically challenged but I still like the changes.

There is something to be said for being happy with the present. It sure does make getting up each day more exciting. If I just wanted to live in the past, I would stay in bed. Now is the time to be alive, so get it together and live it. I don't want to relive the past; I would just rather anticipate the future.

## *Who Killed the Cat?*

Oscar the cat is dead. The cause of death is unknown but unnamed sources say the cat may have been murdered. Now why would anyone want to kill a cat? Well, in this case it might be just the slightest bit understandable.

Oscar was known as the "death cat." He lived in a nursing home and it was reported that when Oscar jumped up on a resident's bed and stayed there that person would soon die. It was written up in all the newspapers and talked about on radio and television shows. I am sure the residents at the nursing home heard about it, too.

So here is this cat that brings with it a hint of death. It creeps down the hall on little cat's paws and spies its next victim. Up on the bed it hops and snuggles down for a wait. The person in the bed is not yet comatose. He or she looks down and the "death cat" is right there, probably grinning like a Cheshire cat. What would any normal person do?

It is reported there was a dented bedpan close to where Oscar was found. No one has claimed responsibility for the act although the name of Osama bin Laden has been mentioned. It was also mentioned the cat was hit eight more times to take care of any other lives that might be lurking within.

What I take away from this incident is how superstitious we all are. I mean, how many of us would have wanted that cat on our bed even though rationally we know the cat couldn't kill? It is a wonder the cat lived as long as it did after the word got out on him.

I have never thought of myself as a person who believed in ghosts or spirits, *but…* We have a two-storey house. Sometimes when I am walking up the stairs, the light will just go on. This has happened over and over. It has gotten to the point that when it happens I say out loud, "Thanks, Mother." My wife and I are both convinced she is protecting us by turning on the light.

Then there is the case of the fan in the baby's room. A couple of years ago, I was trying to change the speed of the fan and the chain broke. So we've not been able to use that fan at all.

Recently it has been so hot that in addition to the air conditioning I have been running all the upstairs fans. I kept wishing the one in the baby's room was working. One day I went in, looked up, and the chain for the fan in that room was attached again. Now I didn't fix it. I wouldn't know how to fix it. My wife says she didn't fix it. This was the kind of thing my father-in-law Joe always did for us.

Joe had not been at our house for a year or more before he died. And now a few months after his death, the fan is fixed. We both think Joe did it. Call us crazy, but we do.

Some people would be psyched out by these events. But I am not. I find comfort in them. They have made a believer out of me. That's the reason I can understand why the cat had to die.

## *An Angry Young Man*

My brother has kept a journal for most of his life. A few months ago he started going back through some of his writings and now sends me some of his stories. Every few mornings, I will wake up, turn on my computer, and there will be a memory from our childhood. The strange thing about these "memories" is they are all from his perspective, which is decidedly different from mine.

Right now, he's sending me stories during the period right after our mother died. Just about all of them concern me and my anger. I lashed out against just about everybody who happened to cross my path. He wrote in his journal that "Jackie had another of his mad spells today." I can tell that he thought I was just spoiled and acting out.

In truth though, I was angry. I was mad at the world. I was mad at God. I was mad at anything and everything. In my opinion my world had been destroyed and I was mad about it. I remember I felt totally frustrated and helpless to do anything about anything. No one had any idea as to how to cope with me and so I just got madder and madder.

I have always used sleep as a retreat from depression or frustration and during that time I slept as much as I could. No one seemed to care that I stayed in my room a lot. So I would go there and go to sleep, and in my sleep state I wasn't angry. In my sleep state I hadn't lost the world. I don't know if this sleep thing works for other people but it did for me.

Eventually I learned to accept the new world that had been forced upon me. I was able to control my anger and keep it under wraps. I halfway became the person I was before my mother died. Still I retained a temper and it would flare up from time to time.

*Memory's Mist*

There is never a right time for tragedy to strike but I think the teen years are the worst. In your teens, especially the early teen years, your emotions are bobbing around inside you like pinballs in a machine. One moment you feel one way and the next you feel entirely different. Add a family tragedy to that situation and you have chaos.

I remember sitting outside at night looking up at the vast sky and wondering why me? I couldn't find an answer to that question. It didn't help to think that death happened to millions of other families day after day. I just knew it had happened to my family and I didn't understand why.

Even today after so many years have passed, I can still think about my mother dying at a young age and leaving two sons behind and I feel the anger stirring inside of me. The emotions have been pushed down, but they are still there. I guess they will never truly go away.

My brother sends me his "memories" and they take me back to a faraway time and a long ago place. And through his words that "angry young man" comes to life again. I understand him and sadly I still grieve for and with him.

## *What Happened to Privacy?*

Maybe it is because I am a South Carolina native, but I am getting sick and tired of the poor Miss South Carolina Teen 2007 being ridiculed and vilified. Okay, she gave a dumb answer to a question posed to her in the Miss Teen USA competition. Big deal. But thanks to YouTube she has been ridiculed over and over again.

That's what happens these days. You make a mistake and someone captures it with a phone or some other kind of electronic devise and then your mistakes, or your sins, are with you forever. Lauren Caitlin, Miss Teen South Carolina, is only eighteen years old. She had a brain freeze, a meltdown, a panic attack, or whatever when she was asked her pageant question. She gave a dumb answer. So what? But now that it has been shown and played on all network and cable channels and has had three million hits on YouTube, the poor girl will be branded dumber than dirt for life.

Not only is it bad that it is being aired on a regular basis, there is also the mean spiritedness that goes with it. The fact that Lauren Caitlin is a very pretty girl just makes people more eager to tear her down. The opinion seems to be that it is okay to hurt her since she is also pretty. That's pathetic.

These days every misstep a person makes can be captured on a cell phone. Everybody is living in a glass house, so there had better be no stones thrown. We learn more about the private lives of celebrities than we need to know or even want to know.

When I was coming along, we had a party line on our phone (Boy, that sounds ancient!). What was amazing is that people were so respectful of another person's privacy that they would hang up if the line was occupied. Today, I think they would stay on the line and take notes.

Honestly, folks, did we really need to hear the full tape of Larry Craig's interview for disorderly conduct? I couldn't listen to it. And do we need to know the infinite details of each and every thing that Brittney, Lindsay, Paris, and Nicole do? I for one am sick of Brangelina, and every other couple combination to come down the pike. I know too much about Gullianni's marriages, Romney's religion, and McCain's age. Ditto for Hillary's home life and Mrs. John Edwards's illness. Just give me their plans for making this country better.

Privacy is not a dirty word and sometimes ignorance is bliss. Being private does not mean you have dirty secrets to hide; it just means you were not brought up to blab about every detail of your life.

Miss Teen South Carolina messed up a question. She didn't rob a store or murder anyone. Give it a rest, people, and let her go on with her young life in peace!

## *All's Well That Ends Well*

Several months ago, my doctor decided it was time for me to have a colonoscopy. It wasn't that he thought there was anything wrong, but that at my age I should have it done. I was not enthused. Still I told him to go ahead and set me up with an appointment with the doctor who did such procedures. He did but it took me a couple of months to get an appointment. These doctors are busy people.

When I finally got to see the "specialist" it was just for the preliminary "get to know each other." This doctor explained what the procedure was and gave me a prescription for the medications I would have to take in advance. The colonoscopy was set up for a date two months later. Nothing about this procedure went fast.

As I awaited the appointment, I began to get advice from my friends who had already had the procedure. Their comments ran from "horrible" to "worst thing ever." All of them seemed to agree that the procedure was not as bad as the preparation for it. Everyone talked about the horrible liquid stuff you have to drink and the volume you have to swallow down. By this time, I was dreading this thing like the plague.

Finally the day before the procedure arrived and I began my fast. I had been told not to eat anything solid that day so my wife had prepared different types of jello and some broths. I could also have all the diet coke I wanted as well as tea. So even that part wasn't too bad. But I was still dreading drinking the prescribed liquids.

When it finally came time to drink the stuff, I was surprised by the taste. It actually tasted like an Alka-seltzer or even a lime or lemon drink. It wasn't bad at all, and this is coming from someone who usually gags over any liquid medicine.

The next morning, my wife and I headed to the hospital for my appointment. At this time I should tell you I am a complete fatalist/hypochondriac. I always think the worst when I have any kind of illness. I have been dying for decades. At this point, I was convinced the doctor would find all kinds of growths in my colon and it would be downhill from that point on. I had planned my funeral, how to tell my kids, finding a new husband for my wife, everything.

On the way to the hospital, my wife and I didn't talk much. She knows how I am and didn't want to encourage any last minute funeral plans. We did have a prayer in order to make sure God knew I was having this procedure. I may be a hypochondriac, but I am a Christian hypochondriac

When it actually came time for the procedure, the doctor told me they were going to give me something to make me relax. I don't know what it was, but it put me out like a light though I did vaguely hear him say "no polyps here."

The next thing I knew they were taking me to the recovery room where he came in and told me and my wife that everything was fine. I was elated, ecstatic, overjoyed. I was back from the brink and could now get on with the rest of my life. It was like getting a new lease on life.

The day before I had actually thought about canceling the procedure. I figured why know if anything was wrong. Ignorance was bliss, right? Wrong. I wouldn't take anything for having this done and getting a clean bill of health.

In retrospect, I would encourage everyone to have this done. It isn't painful, it isn't traumatic, it isn't even bothersome. I will go back in ten years and have it done again, and I won't dread it at all.

All's well that ends well, and I feel a heck of a lot better today than before I had it done.

## *A Happy Birthday*

When I was small (pre-teen), I loved my birthdays. They were always times of excitement and fun. But after my mother died, any type of holiday or celebration lost its charm. I just preferred my birthday be treated like any other day and I was happiest when I could go on with the routine of my life.

After I got married, this attitude of mine used to drive my wife crazy. She is big on birthdays and likes to celebrate them. So I tried to dredge up some enthusiasm especially after our boys were born and they wanted to celebrate. Still inside I would rather just let the day pass without any fanfare.

Last Thursday was my birthday. My wife was at work and I had agreed to go to Tifton to take part in the Governor's Conference on Tourism. My wife and some friends said it was a shame I had to be working on my birthday. I left the house with a smile on my face. It was a day like any other, and there was no celebration planned.

On that Thursday, I shared a booth with fellow authors Bonnie Cella and Amy Blackmarr. We talked with the people who were attending the conference, told them a little bit about Georgia authors, and even sold a few books. It was a great day—no, a grand day. I like being able to meet new people and learn about what they do. I like having people ask me about my writing as well as about my weekly radio show. It is fun, and it is part of the routine of my life.

On Saturday, my wife and I went to Moultrie to see my son, daughter-in-law and grandchildren. We grilled steaks and had potatoes and salad with them. Then we had a chocolate chip cookie with a candle stuck in the middle of it. I was presented with a new pair of khaki shorts as well as Tim McGraw's new CD. I had a wonderful time because it was a gathering not on my birthday.

*Memory's Mist*

On Sunday, my wife made my favorite dinner of roast beef cooked with little potatoes, carrots, and onions. It was delicious. I ate myself silly and I enjoyed every bite. It was a super meal on a day that was not my birthday.

In October, we are going to make a trip to Durham to see my son and daughter-in-law. I have been told we will celebrate my birthday. I know I will enjoy it because it will take place on a day that's not my birthday.

Does all of this sound a little bit crazy? Probably. But I am who I am, and I am a person who gets sad on any holiday or celebration. Call it my sentimental Southern side, or just call it stupid, but don't try to force me to be a joyful person on these days. I will celebrate on the off days and be as personable and charming as possible. It is kind of wacky but it is the way I want to be.

By the way a friend sent me a caramel cake to help me celebrate. I got it the day before my birthday so that was fine. And it was fine again the day after my birthday.

## *The Accidental Author*

I have been a published writer now for eight years, and I still can't believe it. There is something strangely bizarre about the whole thing. Now don't get me wrong, I have always loved to write. I wrote in high school for our newspaper and I did so in college, but that was just having fun with words. I never in my wildest dreams thought I could be a "writer."

Well, passing my time through life I had other occupations such as lawyer, personnel director, movie critic, etc. I still review movies but I have let the other careers go. They didn't satisfy whatever need there was in me. Then came writing and I do believe it is what I was born to do.

I became a published writer by accident. At the time, I knew several writers. Jackie White, Ed Williams, and Milam McGraw Probst were the three who influenced me the most. They were published writers and to me they were icons. I was in awe of them.

For years I have been keeping a daily journal of sorts. I write down full stories or just snippets of ideas, but I write down something every day. When a reporter friend of mine told me I should try to get the stories from these daily journals published, my three friends encouraged me every step of the way. They were there when I sent out five letters to a variety of small publishers. They were there when one showed an interest. They are still here and are my close friends to this day.

Once I began this accidental career, I had the chance to meet more and more writers. They have all been supportive and encouraging. One of the most important people in my writing career is St. John Flynn. St. John is the host of Georgia Public Broadcasting's *Cover to Cover*.

## Memory's Mist

When my first book, *Journey of a Gentle Southern Man*, was published, St. John asked me to come to Atlanta and record some of my stories for *Georgia Gazette*, a weekly radio program on GPB. Having my stories read on the air made my name better known than anything else possibly could have—okay, maybe Oprah would have brought me more fame, but let's talk reality.

Later St. John invited me to be the guest writer on *Cover to Cover*. Now, the man is either delusional or he thought it would be a hoot to have someone on to talk about writing who doesn't have a clue as to how his career came about. But I went on the show and St. John asked only questions I could answer. That's his brilliance: he knows how to particularly interview each person he has as a guest. I mean, he couldn't ask Terry Kay and me the same questions.

Speaking of Terry Kay, there is another idol of mine. When I signed with Mercer University Press after my second book had been published, they agreed to publish my third book *Halfway Home*. They also asked me who I wanted to write the introduction. I didn't have a clue. They then asked me who my favorite author was and the name Terry Kay immediately came to mind. So ask him, they told me.

I had Terry's e-mail address or I got it from his website. I sent him a three paragraph e-mail telling him why he shouldn't write my introduction. I told him he was too busy, too famous, too tired, too kind, and a million other things. Then I sent it to him. He replied immediately and said he would do it. Now that's class!

Through the years I have met people like Patti Callahan Henry who just exudes encouragement. She has a group around her that includes Mary Alice Monroe, Marjory Wentworth, and Patti Morrison. They all adopted me and made me feel like a part of their world.

Yes, I came into this world of writing by accident but since I have landed I have never felt so secure. Writers are good people. I have yet to see a competitive streak among authors. I have other writers telling me all the time about book festivals, bookstores, and the like. They offer suggestions as to how I can make my books better known.

I love this life; I love this world; I love these people. Everyone has a story in them. I just hope everybody gets the chance to tell his or hers like I have been able to do.

## *Grieve Well, Heal Well*

A few days ago, I attended a memorial service held by the veterans' hospital where my father-in-law was during the end of his illness. The services are held every four months and honor those who died at the hospital during that time.

I was amazed at the number of people listed on the program. It seems we are losing a large number of veterans across the country at a rapid rate. Of course, with the new conflicts around the world that number will be increasing.

At the service, each name of the veterans was read and as it was spoken a candle was lit in his or her honor. When all the names had been read and all the candles lit, the people conducting the service stepped back and the lights of the candles spelled out "Hope." It was very touching and inspiring.

One of the speakers at the service was a lady who works with hospice. She made several points about grief and how to handle it. One of the most impressive was that you have to grieve well in order to heal well. This simple statement really hit home to me. I mean, how do you grieve well?

Then she discussed how some of us think it is weak to show emotion and therefore keep it all inside. She said tears are healing and are a natural part of grieving. She also said we have to give ourselves the right to say good-bye.

Saying good-bye does not mean forgetting; it simply means moving on with your life. I have heard people say over and over that after the death of a loved one they felt guilty every time they laughed. It was like they were being disloyal. Now, if we really think about it, if someone loved us would they want us to be gloomy and sad forever more? I don't think so.

I remember after my mother died, the first time I went to a party and had a good time some of my acquaintances looked at me like I was a terrible person. It's the whole sackcloth and ashes thing. Some people want to see an outward showing of grief. I didn't ascribe to that as I knew my mother would want me to enjoy my life.

Then there is the packing up of stuff that belonged to the deceased. For some of us it can be a long time before we want to do something like that, whereas for others it can be an immediate need. I have a friend who has kept his home like a shrine to his dead wife. I keep thinking he can't get on with his life as long as he is stuck in the past. I try to tell him that moving forward is not an abandonment, but I haven't convinced him yet.

For our own emotional well-being, we need to "heal well." Sadness and grief can lead to actual physical illnesses. My belief is you grieve as strongly as you need to and then you move on. You don't forget, but you move on.

If you have lost someone and are grieving, or if you know someone who is, think about that simple phrase—you have to grieve well in order to heal well. Maybe in some way it will help. I hope so.

## *You Gotta, Gotta Have Friends*

Friends are very important to me, always have been and always will be. But lately I feel I give my friends the short end of the stick. There are just not enough hours in the day to communicate and spend time with them like I want to do. By the time I spend time with my wife, check on my children and grandchildren, and keep my career afloat, there's very little time left for my friends.

Before I got married, my life was nothing but friends. I was constantly with them, constantly talking to them. I helped solve their problems and they helped solve mine. Then I got married and my friendships changed. I just didn't have the time or the inclination to spend as much time with them. Some of my friends understood and accepted the changed relationship; others didn't and the friendships ended.

In my pre-marriage days, I was a "fixer." I was the person you came to with your problems and I would work to solve them. If you were having problems with your job, I was always there to make a suggestion. If you were having trouble in your relationships, I would offer advice. People came in and out of my apartment constantly and my phone was always ringing. I loved it.

After I got married, the phone continued to ring and people continued to drop by, until my wife told me to fix it. That meant I had to tell people I was not available like I had been. I hated doing it. It was like pulling teeth and it hurt. It hurt me and it hurt them.

After awhile, I found you could have friendships that were not totally consuming. My wife and I made friends with other couples, and I still managed to have some single friends. These relationships have enriched my life and I wouldn't trade them for anything.

But life is complicated and time goes by faster and faster. As you get older, you spend more time worrying about your parents, making sure your kids are okay, and having cherished time with your grandkids. One of my sons lives an hour and a half away and my wife and I can get in the car and go to see him and his family whenever we want. My other son and his wife live in Durham. That's seven and a half hours away. That's quite a trip.

Would I like to see them often? Sure I would. But it seems like blocking out that much time for a visit gets harder and harder to do. I am doing a lot of speaking to groups and I hate to say no. I enjoy doing this. Plus there is my commitment to be on television and the radio once a week. I also write entertainment reviews for several newspapers. That takes up a lot of my time.

So where does that leave my friends? Well, some of them I see at church, some of them I have lunch with every once in a while, but none of them do I see as often as I like. There are some good people in this world and my friends fall into that group.

I figure this lack of time is going to be a problem until the day I die. It is not a bad problem to have, but it is a worrisome one. I want to be a good friend. I hope my friends except the quality of the time I give them if not the quantity.

## *Fathers and Sons*

Recently a friend of mine's father died and it was decided my friend should give the eulogy. My friend agreed to do it somewhat reluctantly because he knew his father would be a hard person to eulogize in a totally positive way.

There had been problems in his relationship with his father. Still he thought maybe some of the complex situations between them might help others know his father in a more understandable way. So he gave the eulogy and he pointed out some of the problems. He did not savage his father but he did try to be honest.

The relationship between fathers and sons are often difficult. I think those between mothers and daughters are usually more difficult, but the male relationship can be a hard one too. My father and I loved each other but I don't know if we ever really knew each other. I was/am a man of many moods and passions. My father knew one mood and that was happy.

On any given day at any given time at any given point in his life, you could ask my father how he was doing and his answer would always be the same. He would tell you he was just fine. How could a man who lost his wife to cancer be fine? How could a man who had cancer himself be fine? How could a man with a million other problems be fine?

One of our biggest problems was that he always thought things were fine. I remember early in my teenage years coming to my father with some sort of problem. It was something that had happened at school. As I began to unburden myself to him, he quickly told me not to tell him. He said it would give him a headache. Later I learned he had an abnormal tolerance for pain and never, ever had headaches.

My father loved being around his family as long as they didn't cause any problems. He didn't like conflict. He didn't like anything that made him feel uncomfortable. After I was grown and married, he would tell me how he liked to visit me and my family. Then he would quickly add that he didn't want us to live in the same town. He didn't want to know the problems of my daily life.

Talking about keeping our distance was one of the few serious conversations I ever had with my father. Usually it was just about who in the family was graduating from school, or who was moving with their job, or something informative but light. He never once asked about my dreams, my aspirations, my highs, or my lows.

I regret that we never had a deep and intense conversation wherein I could get to know him and he could get to know me. I blame myself for this failure as much as I blame him. I should have forced the issue. He went to his grave being a sweet, lovable man who was always fine.

When my father died I gave his eulogy. I talked about how much he was liked and how happy he was. I talked about how I would miss him and how the whole community would, too. I said only positive things. But maybe I should have asked some of the people who were there what he was really like. Who was my father when he was not around me? Did he open up to anyone and let them see who he really was?

I talk to my two sons just about every day. I try to be as honest with them as possible. I don't want them to one day realize they didn't know their father at all—like I did.

## *It's Dangerous to Be Sick*

A friend of mine has been having problems with his knees lately. One of them got so bad that he agreed to have a total knee replacement. I was concerned about this because he is divorced and lives alone. I worried about the surgery, about the after-surgery treatment, and then how he would fare when he came home.

I have had people tell me over and over that in this day and age if you don't have someone with you at the hospital when you are sick, you will be in a heap of trouble. These people have told me you need a family member or friend to be with you for the duration of your stay in order to make sure you are taken good care of by the hospital staff. Luckily I have not been hospitalized recently so I don't know if it is true or not. However I believed it enough to be concerned for my friend.

The surgery was a success. He was a little groggy but otherwise doing okay. The next morning, it was a different story. During the night, his temperature went up to 103 degrees and his heart started racing. The staff gave him some medication and it helped, thank goodness.

What amazed me was that none of his doctors ever explained to him the reason for the fever and/or the heart palpitations. They brushed off his inquiries or laughed it off. Later my friend's eyes began to burn and became sticky. He thought he had pink eye but the hospital gave him some eye medication again without any explanation.

After two days, my friend was supposed to be moved to a rehabilitation facility—but there was no room available. And there was no room the next day or the next day. Finally the doctor came in and asked if my friend wanted to go to rehab or go home. My friend answered that he wanted to do whatever was best for his knee. After assurances he would get physical therapy at home, my friend checked out of the hospital.

When he got home, he had a health care assistant coming in four hours each day. She came the first day and tried to do as much as she could, but she only spoke a small amount of English. This meant in addition to having a bum knee and some pain, my friend also had to try to communicate with the woman sent to assist him at home.

Hopefully, his knee will get stronger, and to tell you the truth, I'm glad he's out of the hospital. With so many scare stories circulating about staph infections, you have to be concerned.

I can remember when hospitals were places of care and service. You got lots of TLC from the beginning of your stay until the end. Today many hospitals are understaffed and overbooked, and you enter at your own risk.

So if you can make arrangements in advance for someone in your family or a friend to check on you. You are going to need some help. No one can be expected to just do it on his own. A lot of people are probably more than willing to give you assistance but are waiting to be asked. Do it. The life you save may be your own.

## *Nature or Nurture*

A few days ago, I was talking with a friend of mine who lives in South Carolina. I asked him how his family was doing and there was a pause. Then my friend asked if I really wanted to know. I assured him that I did, and he began to tell me a lengthy story of family woes.

My friend, who I will call Gus, is in his mid-forties. He got married right out of college and he and his wife had three sons. After the third one was born, Gus's wife went off the deep end. She got involved with drugs and left Gus and his boys and moved to California. A few years later, Gus married again. This time it was to a woman who shared his values.

Kate, Gus's wife, has been the only mother his boys have ever known. She has loved them and cared for them like they were naturally born to her. She and Gus have raised them in the church and have set good examples of what clean-living, hard-working people should be. Gus is with the forestry service and makes good if not great money. He and his family have lived comfortably.

Their oldest son finished college and got a job in Oklahoma. He and his wife and family live out there and are doing fine. The middle son joined the Army out of high school and was killed in a helicopter crash a few months after he entered service. The third son, well, he has been a problem for years.

David, the youngest son, always expected more and more from Gus and Kate. He was never satisfied. If they bought him a car, he wanted a different one. If they joined the country club so he could play golf, he wanted to belong to a better one. Nothing was good enough for David, and then he got involved with drugs.

Gus said he was stupid and didn't see it coming. He knew David was always out of money, but he thought he was just wasting it. Then he noticed that he wasn't hanging around with his old friends. And then there was the night David was arrested for drug possession.

David, of course, had a perfectly good excuse for why he had the drugs. They weren't his, and he had just been in the wrong place at the wrong time. Gus hired a good but costly lawyer who got the charges reduced. Gus said he told David over and over how lucky he was.

Things went from bad to worse after this. It ended when Gus found out David had stolen his ATM card and almost emptied the bank account. When he confronted David, he denied doing it. David seemed to have little knowledge about how ATM surveillance cameras record each patron.

When Gus called the police to file charges against David they told him he didn't need to. There were outstanding warrants against him in other counties. This time the charges weren't reduced and now David is in a "gated" community and wears an orange uniform.

Gus and Kate are distraught. They don't know how he could have turned out this way. They honestly tried to do everything right—and it worked with the other two boys. But maybe David inherited a weakness for drugs from his mother. Maybe it was totally genetic.

Gus asked me what I thought and I absolutely don't know the answer. I have seen good people struggling with messed-up kids and I have seen messed-up parents have exceptional children. I told Gus that you just have to do the best you can and pray it all works out.

Nature versus nurture? Who knows? It seems it's all the toss of the coin. There are no guarantees in life. My wife and I worked hard to raise our kids the "right way" and I think it paid off. But it could have had another outcome. Hearing Gus's story made me realize just how fortunate we are.

## *Dumpster Dating*

Dumpster dating—have you ever heard that phrase before? I hadn't until a few days ago. I belong to an Internet group and one of the members was talking about someone dating a skanky girl. And that's when the term dumpster dating was used. It isn't a nice thing to say about someone, but in a few case it is what truly applies

We have all had friends who have toppled head over heels for the wrong guy or girl. I knew a girl who was just the nicest person in the world but she had this thing for bad boys. I mean her radar could hone in on them from a hundred miles away. She dated drunks, druggies, morally polluted guys and she always seemed in shock when they broke her heart.

Her best friends tried to talk to her. Her parents tried to reason with her. Her pastor even got into the act. But she was oblivious to anything and everything that was said to her. Her favorite phrase was "the heart knows what the heart knows." I didn't even know what that meant but she took it to mean that you follow your heart no matter where it leads you. In her case, it was down the road to destruction.

Eventually this girl married one of these dumpster dudes and had a couple of kids. She finally got the message of what a loser he was when he beat her up in front of the children. She left him then and moved back home. She raised her kids and has had a fairly happy life. But it is a life alone. After a series of losers, she no longer trusts herself to make wise choices.

When a person is dating someone you know is bad for them should you speak up? I have known parents who choked on their tongues from not speaking up. In some instances their silence paid off since their child came to his/her senses on his or her own. In other cases, the parents saw their child go into a terrible situation.

In one specific case, I remember the parents voiced their opinion and their daughter still married the guy. The families stayed estranged because the guy could never forget what his in-laws had said. Maybe in that case they would have been better off biting their tongues.

In another case, the parents constantly harassed their son about the girl he was dating. They didn't say he was dumpster dating, they just said she was trash. Eventually they did persuade him to drop her. But the next girl he dated was even worse—and he married her.

To speak or not to speak, that's the question. Fortunately, I have perfect daughters-in-law so I never had that problem. Plus to my knowledge I never dated anyone of whom my parents didn't approve. Still there might have been some parents out there who didn't want their daughters dating Jackie Cooper. I just hope they didn't say I was a dumpster date.

## *One Door Shutting*

Now, this has been a week. I started out on top of the world, just having a good time with all the great elements of my life. My family, my friends, my career—it was all going great. Then I got a phone call. It was from the new program director for Georgia Public Broadcasting's radio division.

This new best friend was calling to tell me that my weekly radio show *Fridays with Jackie* was being cancelled. As I sputtered and gulped, I managed to ask why. His response was the show had no focus. Then he added that since it was on during *Morning Edition* on Fridays it had to possess a certain level of content and sadly *FWJ* didn't rise to the challenge.

That was it. Seventeen months after this venture started it was over. Shot down in the prime of life. Was I angry? You bet. Was I embarrassed? Even more so. Was I surprised? Yes, and that's where I was an idiot. I honestly believed that if you gave your heart and soul to something and presented it with sincerity it would work.

When I first presented the idea of *Fridays with Jackie* to St. John Flynn, I did so to help publicize all the creative people in Georgia. I wanted to talk about Terry Kay and Steve Berry but I also wanted to talk about Jackie White and Dale Cramer. The big names will always have their time in the sun, but the ones who are not quite at that top rung sometimes get overlooked.

So during these seventeen months we have had the opportunity to do just that. And my gosh has the reception been overwhelming. As I have gone around the state speaking to different groups, I have been bombarded with comments from people who said they tuned in every week. Then there was the most frequently asked question, "What is St. John Flynn really like?" The answer, "Your guess is as good as mine."

The second most stated comment always tickled me. People would say, "You must be making the big bucks now." Yeah, sure. It cost me to do the show. I did not get paid. It was a voluntary thing from the start. For the first year I drove to Atlanta from Perry each week to record the show and that costs money. Later I was able to go to Macon to tape.

Money wasn't the motivator. It was a labor of love. It was something that was fun to do and it was also very rewarding to my spirit. Plus St. John is great fun to work with and I enjoyed his dry sense of humor. I really do think *Fridays with Jackie* showed a side of him that never came through on *Cover to Cover*.

So now that it has been cancelled, do I regret doing it? Absolutely not. I had a wonderful time. Plus the e-mails and comments I have gotten since word got out that it had been cancelled have been terrifically gratifying.

One door has closed, but I am sure another one will open. It won't be on Georgia Public Broadcasting, but there are other venues. So stay tuned. Life is a journey and I feel there are more paths left to follow in my life.

## *Off to the Beach*

This year I decided my wife and I would celebrate Thanksgiving in a different way. Usually she spends her time in the kitchen cooking up a big celebratory meal. And usually we have the kids and grandkids home to eat. Well, this year my oldest son and his wife are expecting their first child so they could not make the trip down from Durham.

My youngest son and his family hadn't contacted us about what their plans were. Usually they eat the noon meal with my daughter-in-law's parents. So when they called to ask what we were doing and saying they were planning on coming to our house, it was too late. We had already made our plans for a Thanksgiving getaway. Friends of ours have a condo at Panama City and they offered it and we accepted. We left town on the Wednesday before Thanksgiving and didn't come back until the Saturday afterwards.

I have always liked the beach in the winter. I am not a water person. I prefer to look at the beach from the balcony of the condo and that's what we did. I didn't even touch the sand or the surf. The weather was warm until Friday and then it dropped like a ton of bricks. I had to make a run to Target and get a sweater.

While there I read two books, reviewed three TV shows, and went to see three movies. There is a new mall being built right across the street from the condo and the movie theater is already open for business. I saw a movie on Wednesday, Thursday, and Friday.

We ate out on Wednesday and Friday, but on Thursday my wife made us hot turkey sandwiches with broccoli casserole, mashed potatoes, and English peas. We even had strawberry shortcake for dessert. We ate it with gusto.

The only problem was the three and a half days went by too quickly. Even me, who loves my routine life, enjoyed this winter vacation. Okay, I was ready to get back and check my e-mail and pick up my mail at the post office, etc. but not obsessively so.

Since my wife's father died this summer, I knew it was gong to be tough on her this holiday season. So a change of scenery and doing the unexpected was a great way to divert her melancholy mood. It worked. I'm not saying she didn't think of her father, but it wasn't the only thing on her mind.

Next year we will probably be back to doing the Thanksgiving thing at our house. By then my new grandbaby should be able to travel, and I will check with my youngest son to make sure we are included in his plans. Still for this year and our trip away to the beach, I am truly thankful.

## *And Then There Were Three*

When I was growing up, I always thought it would have been neat to have had a sister. It was just my brother and myself and I knew my parents planned no more children. Then when my brother grew up and married he had two sons and then a daughter.

Afterwards, I thought maybe I would have a daughter after my two sons. But after my two boys were born, my wife and I decided not to have any more children. My "daughter" was missing in action. This was really disappointing to me as I had always wanted a daughter to name after my deceased mother.

Eventually my youngest son got married and I finally had a "daughter." Well, at least I had a daughter-in-law! Then they had a baby and it was a girl! To add the cherry on top they named her Genna after my mother Virginia. She was the girl I had been waiting for all my life and she was the first grandchild, so how special can you get?

Two years later they had another child and this one was a boy. His name is Walker Cooper and he is special in his own way. He is the most laid back child I have ever seen. Nothing ruffles him. He just goes his own way at his own pace. He is always good-natured and always loving. He is great!

Walker is also one of those children who wears clothes perfectly. They just fit exactly right on his body. I have always been one of those people who fights his clothes. They are too small or too large, but never just right. You could put Walker in a sack suit and on him it would look good.

So here I was with two grandchildren and lo and behold I found out we were going to have number three. JJ, my oldest son, took his sweet time in getting married. But he finally met the right girl and tied the knot. Angela, his wife, is Chinese so when they told us they were expecting, my wife and I began to look closely at all Asian babies we saw.

Their baby was supposed to be born on December 20 but she arrived early on November 27, and only after a couple of false alarms. She is just beautiful with a full head of black hair and the sweetest face you have ever seen. She definitely looks like her mother and that's just fine with me. She is my China doll.

We are going to see her this weekend. JJ's family lives in Durham, North Carolina, so it's a long ride. Still when you are going to see a new grandbaby, the miles will fly by. I hope she's just as excited about the thought of seeing us.

It is amazing how things can change in an instant. Before November 27, we talked about this baby in the abstract, now we constantly talk about how much she sleeps, how much she eats, does she cry, etc. Natalie Michelle Cooper is always in our thoughts.

Natalie has settled into the middle of my heart, right between Genna and Walker. It is a perfect fit and there is plenty of room for even more grandchildren should that be God's will. A few weeks ago there were two and now there are three. I am brimful with happiness.

## *Travels with Jackie*

This past weekend we went to Durham to see Baby Natalie, our newest grandchild. We didn't leave for Durham until 3:30 in the afternoon because I had a booksiging. The trip to Durham is at least seven hours if you stop to eat and so we pulled in to my son's house around eleven that night.

Now I know I am still in my prime, but driving for seven hours takes it out of you. Then by the time we got to our motel, it was after midnight. When I tried to sleep, I felt like I was still driving the car. Yep, I drove most of the night.

The next day was spent with Natalie. We went to her house around nine in the morning and stayed until ten that night. For some reason, I didn't sleep very good that night either and the next morning we awoke, got dressed, and hit the road. Seven hours later we were finally home. I have never been so happy to see our house.

Natalie is a beautiful baby. She smells sweet and feels soft and cuddly. She actually woke up a little Sunday afternoon and charmed us all. We got to see her eyes and watch her smile. Okay, it may have been gas…but she still smiled.

JJ, his wife Angela, and Natalie will be down here for Easter, but that seems like a long time away. I may just have to crank up the car and head north one more time. Seven hours isn't really that bad.

Today I headed to Albany, Georgia, to visit the set of the movie *Fireproof*. This is the latest movie being made by the folks at Sherwood Baptist Church. Their first film was *Flywheel* which is now available on DVD. Their second was the fantastically successful *Facing the Giants*, which gained national release and acclaim.

The folks at Sherwood Baptist write, direct, and act in their movies. They handle all the jobs, even the technical ones, with very little outside help. Alex and Stephen Kendrick, associate ministers at the church, wrote the script for *Fireproof*. Alex is also the director and Stephen is the producer.

Kirk Cameron is the star of the film. He plays a firefighter whose marriage is in trouble. I got a chance to talk with him and he told me he had seen *Facing the Giants* and was so impressed he contacted Alex and told him he would be happy to help with any future films. He then got a phone call asking if he would like to audition for this movie. I was totally surprised they would ask Kirk Cameron to audition. He said it didn't upset him as he knew Alex sees each film as a mission and testimony and he has to make sure the actors are completely right for the roles talentwise and spiritually.

*Fireproof* should wrap up filming this week and then the editing process begins, which Alex says is his favorite part of the process. The film has been a labor of love for all involved and as for its future success? Well, it is in God's hands.

## *My Uncle Frank*

In this day and age when heroes seem to be in short supply, I think back to those who I considered heroic when I was growing up. The name that's always at the top of my list is my Uncle Frank. He was my mother's sister's husband and their family also lived in Clinton, South Carolina, where I grew up.

Uncle Frank was a housing contractor, but he was also a trained bricklayer. I could take you around Clinton to this day and show you houses my Uncle Frank built. He was also a churchgoer. In all my years growing up in the First Baptist Church of Clinton, my Uncle Frank was there every Sunday. I don't remember a time he missed. He wasn't a man who discussed his religion; he just lived it.

He also was a man who many people called Maggie. You read that right. His nickname was Maggie and I never knew why. It wasn't used in a derisive or derogatory way by anyone. It was just a name he was called. I regret that I never asked him or my father why he was called by that name.

The most outstanding image I have in my mind of my Uncle Frank concerned his laying brick. One summer when I was eight or nine he built a house across the street from us. He built it during the summer and I was usually over at the site watching him lay brick or do other things. He could do everything, but I was particularly fascinated by the way he layed brick.

He would take his trowel and scoop up the wet mortar and slap it on the line where the bricks were going. Then he would take the tip of the trowel and make an indention down the middle of the mortar. Next he would take the brick, tamp it down onto the mortar and then scrape away the excess that oozed over the sides from the force of the brick coming down. To me it was like watching someone conduct a symphony. It was that precise and beautiful.

One day that summer, there was a report that a bad windstorm was headed our way. We had those fairly often in Clinton and many times they were accompanied by rain and lightning. Anyway Uncle Frank sent his crew home, but he stayed. He said he had to get two rows of brick layed before he quit. My mother came over to get me and begged Uncle Frank to come to our house and wait out the storm, but he declined.

I went home and got a chair and set it up at our front window where I would have a clear view of him laying brick. The wind came and it was howling. It seemed like some of the trees on Holland Street were bending double, but Uncle Frank never stopped laying brick. He never even looked up at the sky. He just kept on doing what he was doing.

When he finished those two rows he went over to his truck, looked my way, and touched the brim of his hat and drove off. Shortly thereafter the storm passed over. The rows of brick were still standing and stand till this day.

Five years later he built another house on Holland Street. This one was for my Daddy and his new wife. Shortly after my mother died they started dating and before a year was up since my mother's death, they were planning their wedding. In the South at that time, no one got married in less than a year after their spouse died. It was considered totally disrespectful.

But my father and his intended planned to marry as soon as their house was finished and it was supposed to be finished at the end of July. My mother had died the previous August. I went to my Uncle Frank and told him I could not stand it if my Daddy got married in less than a year. He said he understood and for me not to worry. He said there was no way he would let that house be finished until the year's anniversary had passed.

My father got married in October. The wedding had been delayed until the house was finished.

My Uncle Frank could stare down a windstorm, and he could answer a young boy's heartfelt request. He is one of my heroes.

## *The Night after Christmas*

As I write this, it is Christmas night. All the packages have been unwrapped and too much food has been eaten. It has been a good day as Christmases go. Most of my family was with us and everyone was in a pretty good mood. The grandkids got most of the toys they wanted and the adults were just happy with the kids being happy.

This Christmas had the potential for being gloomy, as it was the first Christmas since my father-in-law died. My wife was putting up a brave front, but in her heart I knew she was still grieving. Her mother was also having a hard time. We went to St. Petersburg, Florida, where she lives and brought her back up to Georgia to be with us. I think it helped both my wife and my mother-in-law to be sharing the holiday.

This was also the first year my oldest son JJ was not with us. He and his wife have a month-old baby girl, so traveling from North Carolina to Georgia was out of the question. As much fun as I had today, there was always that empty spot with JJ missing. He promised they would be here next year.

The best thing about this Christmas was it gave me a chance to reflect on my life. I mentally made a list of how blessed I am. I don't know many people who are happier than I am. My family is a constant source of happiness to me. Both of my sons are people I would want to be friends with even if we were not related. My daughters-in-law are both amazingly loving and intelligent women. And my grandchildren, well, they are nearly perfect.

My wife is the only person I know who totally understands me. I would rather watch a movie with her than anyone. She and I are on the same wavelength in just about everything. I love her sense of humor, her warmth, her parenting skills, and a million other things about her. She is my soulmate pure and simple.

*Memory's Mist*

Then there are my friends. I have the best friends possible and we have been friends for ages. We have shared experiences and have stayed friends throughout the years. We have cared for each other's children and now we are involved in the excitement of grandchildren. We share the same basic morals, goals, and faith. We like each other and we like to be with each other.

My faith is still strong. I like attending my church. I like my pastor, and I like the congregation. I like being in a family of faith. There is a comfort in being with people of like faith and it's eased the pain of certain life experiences.

On this Christmas night of 2007, I am a happy and contented man. Life is good and I appreciate it. I am a blessed man.

*Reflections from Route 2008*

## *Be Aggressive*

My brother is the only other member of my original family who is still alive. There were only two of us children in my family along with my mother and father. My mother died when I was fourteen and my father died about six years ago. So now it is just me and my brother who remember the Clinton days growing up.

But lately my brother's health has not been so good. He had to have knee replacement surgery about three months ago and it has been a nightmare. I had known people who had both knees done in a matter of months and they bounced right back. My brother only had one knee done and he hasn't bounced back yet.

The problem in my opinion is he belongs to an HMO. I just don't care for that concept and I feel like he hasn't gotten the best treatment because of it. He swears he has never had any problems in the past and that this time is the exception. I tell him I don't care if it is the exception. He's not getting good medical care.

His knee has been swollen since the surgery. He still can not straighten his leg out completely. He's still in a great deal of pain. Added to that, a couple of weeks ago one of the doctors he sees mentioned that the infection in his leg wasn't serious. Serious! He didn't even know he had an infection.

A week or so later, he saw another doctor who told him the clot in his leg wasn't serious. Clot! He didn't even know he had a clot. Are you getting my drift here? The next thing I know they will be telling him the gangrene isn't serious. Infection or clot, to my mind these are serious issues. They haven't put him on a blood thinner or an antibiotic.

I keep telling him he has to get aggressive with his doctors, but he is of the old school that thinks doctors can do no wrong. Me, I'm skeptical. These guys are human beings and are therefore capable of mistakes. I also think the squeaky wheel gets attention and he ought to be squeaking pretty loudly in order to get their attention.

He finally promised me today that he is going to demand to be seen by his doctor. The last time he saw him he was told to come back in three months. He is going to demand to be seen as soon as possible. I have helped him compile a list of questions to ask and get answered.

I consider this whole business serious. As the voice of doom and gloom, I mention he could lose his leg or even lose his life. I know he hates when I call him and begin on stuff like this. I just see him as a possible victim. He is divorced and lives alone. He doesn't have someone advocating for him like my wife does for me, and I do for her. He has got to take care of himself.

The Hippocratic Oath says, "First do no harm." Doesn't it then say something like "do everything necessary to get your patient well"? I want action because, believe me, this patient's brother is running out of patience.

## *The More We Get Together*

This morning a song was going through my head, "The more we get together, together, together. / The more we get together the happier we'll be." Now I haven't sung that since I was eight or nine but today it came back to me. I guess the reason is that lately I have been getting together more.

For years I would drive through the local fast food restaurant in the mornings and I would see older men sitting around talking and drinking coffee. I always wondered what they were talking about because they were there day after day. It seemed to me they would run out of things to talk about at some point.

But now I have become one of them. No, I don't sit around in the morning but I have found a group of my contemporaries who eat lunch together every day and I go a couple of times a week. I join in the talk about politics, movies, sports, and the war. I have been doing this for the past few months and the talk never even slows down. There is always something to talk about.

In this group there is a judge, two lawyers, a retired military man, a store manager, an engineer, and me. The ages range from forty till death. We are a diverse group, but everyone enjoys all the others. We don't agree on a lot of things, but we do agree that we all like to talk.

This communication thing seems to be bigger than ever. I know people who spend hours each day blogging with a bunch of people they have never met. And among the kids it is text messaging. What a mania that is. A friend of mine told me she took her daughter and a bunch of her friends to a ballgame. On the way back you could have heard a pin drop in the car. Now that's not what I would expect to happen when you get a group of teenage girls together. But this group instead of talking was text messaging. They were texting their friends and even each other (the better for the adult not to be able to hear).

We all have an innate need to communicate. I know it is true with me. I spend a lot of time at my computer writing. That's a lonely activity and some time I do it for days on end. When I stop and go to meet friends and talk I get a rush. My mood immediately lifts and things are better. I don't know if there is actually some fluid that's transmitted by your body when you communicate, but something gives you a charge.

My wife and I have always been talkers. We have these marathon conversations that we call cleaning closets. They help clear the air and keep us on an even keel. I think that's why our marriage is so good—we talk to each other.

You know, it's amazing how the things we learned in childhood really do carry through the years. That childhood song said it all. The more we get together with friends and communicate the happier we will be. At least that's true for me.

## *See Ya, St. John*

Ladies and gentlemen, St. John Flynn has left the building. Yes, after a decade or more of being the voice of Georgia Public Broadcasting, St. John Flynn has resigned. He is moving on to greener pastures and that's a loss for all of Georgia.

For those who for some reason or other might not recognize the name, he is the man who created *Cover to Cover* for GPB. He also appeared in fundraisers for the station and for many years was the voice of local news and events on the Georgia segments of *Morning Edition*. To put it quite simply, to many people he was Georgia Public Broadcasting.

I first came to know St. John as a friend when he asked me to record some stories from my first book *Journey of a Gentle Southern Man* for *Georgia Gazette*. Then when my second book was published, he asked me to do the same thing again. I also was invited to appear twice on *Cover to Cover*.

*Cover to Cover* was one of the most influential broadcast programs in Georgia. Authors coveted the chance to appear on the show because St. John had a loyal listening audience of book devotees. An appearance there guaranteed an increase in book sales as well as widespread exposure for your name and product. The show was only on once a month and there was always a repeat show in December. This means only eleven authors got the nod each year so it was a pretty select group.

Since *Cover to Cover* was St. John's creation, I would assume his departure means that program has ended. St. John's personality and professionalism would be hard to equal, so anyone trying to step into his shoes would have a daunting task.

A year ago I suggested a program to St. John called *Fridays with Jackie*. We got it on the air and taped it each week. It was only a five-minute segment inserted into Morning Edition on Friday mornings, but we had a lot of fun with it. This show allowed St. John's sense of humor to emerge. He wasn't so formal and people responded.

After GPB cancelled the show, I missed having the chance to talk with St. John each week. He is such a knowledgeable person that I missed picking his brain about different people, places, and events. And now he will be gone to greener pastures and communicating with him will be even more difficult.

The arts in Georgia are taking a beating. It's happening in newspapers, magazines, television, and radio shows. The value of our artists is not recognized. St. John Flynn was one of our most worthy assets and now we have let him slip away. We won't be able to replace him and what he brought to the cultural landscape of Georgia.

I know many, many people will miss his voice on the air as he announced that it was once again time for *Cover to Cover* or "civer to civer" as he said it. They will also miss his performances with symphonies around the state as their narrator for some of their events. He also served as master of ceremonies for various awards and benefits. He is a man of many talents and master of all.

It is hard for me to accept the fact St. John Flynn is leaving GPB. Those pastures better be a lot greener to justify him leaving our state behind. Still, I wish him well on all of his new endeavors. He deserves only the best.

Finally, all I can say to him is what I used to say at the end of *Fridays with Jackie* each week. He would say he would see me next week and I would say, "See ya, St. John!"

## *Is the Building the Church?*

A few months ago, I was having a conversation with a friend. He was putting forth the argument that you don't have to attend a church service in a building in order to communicate with God. He said you can feel just as close or closer to Him away from the structured service. I responded by saying this was a cop out and that you need the community of believers in order to maintain and grow in your spiritual life.

That was then and this is now. I am now on the "outs" with my church for reasons I won't go into here and I don't think I can go back for a while. That leaves me on the outside looking in as there is no other church in my area that I want to attend. I like a traditional church service so that leaves me out where the new contemporary churches are. I also don't believe in predestination (bye-bye Presbyterians) or like to hear burn in hell orators (bye-bye Baptists).

My problem is not that I can't communicate with God outside of church; my problem is I like church. I like the rituals and the music. I like sitting in the pews with my family and friends. I like a really good sermon that my pastor was known to deliver. I like it all.

Plus I get chockful of guilt when I don't go to church. Blame it on my mother, but she always stressed Sunday morning was for church. So I can just see me laying around on a Sunday morning feeling guilty as sin about not being up and dressed and in church.

Not only do I like church, I like Sunday school. That's when I got to see my churchgoing friends that I hadn't seen during the week. I liked catching up and then sitting with them as we heard a lesson about life and living.

I am not withdrawing my membership from my church. I am not about to do anything as radical as that. I just plan to lay low for now and maybe for a couple of years. When things change maybe I will return. At least I plan to. I can't imagine spending the rest of my life without it.

For now, I am going back to talk with that friend who told me you don't need the organized church. Maybe he has more information I can use. And maybe he can tell me how and why he doesn't feel guilty every Sunday morning.

## *You've Got to Have Sleep*

I don't know if it is my age, my life, my diet, or what but lately I have had a horrible time falling to sleep. There is a vicious cycle when you don't sleep. Number one, it's all you think about. You wonder if this will be the night when you actually sleep all the way though and wake up refreshed. Then when it comes time to go to bed, you panic. Am I going to sleep, or am I not going to sleep? And lately I don't.

My problem is I fight sleep. I actually get sleepy around eight o'clock at night. But who wants to go to bed at eight o'clock! Still I lull myself into thinking if I am sleepy at eight I will be plumb catatonic at eleven. It doesn't happen that way. Sometime between eight and eleven a point is crossed and I become wide awake.

My wife tells me not to get up when I am not sleeping because as long as I am lying down I am resting. So I lay there and worry about everything that has gone on that day, and what will happen tomorrow, and what happened in the past year. I review it all and try to solve all the problems.

Usually I end up getting on the floor by our bed. I get a blanket and cover myself up and stick my head right in front of the electric fan that runs year round in our bedroom. Sometimes the sound of the fan and the rush of the wind lulls me to sleep, but not always. Still I am comfortable on the floor and I am not tossing around bothering my wife.

When I was a child, I could fall asleep at the drop of a hat. I especially liked sleeping in the late afternoon. That was the best sleep ever. I enjoyed those kind of naps into my adulthood. Before I got married, I would rush home from work, jump in the bed and sleep for a couple of hours. Then I woke up and I was ready for the night.

I have always been a night person. I like to work at night. I certainly write better at night. My thought processes seem to kick in during the evening hours. When I was in college and law school, one of my favorite things was to have deep-rooted discussions late at night into the early morning.

It has been proven that in order to be healthy you have to have sleep. In the tragic case of actor Heath Ledger, he had been having trouble sleeping. He was taking drugs to try to make him sleep. I don't want to go that route. I am still trying hot baths and natural remedies.

I have cut out caffeine at night, well, most caffeine. I still drink diet cokes and I guess they have some caffeine in them. I also am trying to keep my mind on serene things before I go to bed. I read some in the current best seller I am reviewing and then let sleep come naturally to me. But it doesn't come! I may sleep for an hour or so and then I wake up.

Maybe tonight will be the night. Maybe this time I will sleep for eight glorious hours. I hope so. I hope so. I hope so.

## *What Are You Doing the Rest of Your Life?*

At some point in our lives we all ask the same question—what am I going to do with the rest of my life? At least I know I did. It came after I had been practicing law for twelve years or so. I woke up one day dreading facing the day and it was a tipping point. I just couldn't do it any longer.

Now that's not to say a legal career can't be a rewarding one, both emotionally as well as monetarily. It can be. I know a lot of lawyers who are happy as clams. I also know a lot who aren't. I also know insurance salesman, car dealers, bankers, and others who wish they had chosen something else.

But the fact of the matter is that most of us can change careers if we really want to take some risks. I know you can't jeopardize your family's stability, but usually new opportunities present themselves and all you have to do is make a leap of faith. That's what I did and I have been a happier person for it. I can still remember though how panic stricken my wife looked when I told her that the legal profession and I were coming to a parting of ways.

I chose law as my profession for all the wrong reasons. I have told this story so often I can do it in my sleep. I was in the eleventh grade and my English teacher asked me what I was going to study in college. When I said I didn't know, she told me to make up my mind by Monday (This was on a Friday.). I went home, turned on the TV, and there was *Perry Mason*. I thought he seemed to be happy, so I picked a legal career.

By the time I began to have doubts, it was too late, or so I felt. My family was gloriously happy they were going to have a lawyer in the family. My high school and college counselors affirmed I was going to have a wonderful career. Everyone was sure about it except me.

Anyway after more than a few years I jumped off the legal express and I haven't looked back with regret a single time since then. Its funny but some young lawyers tell me I am their main hope for happiness in their careers. They tell themselves if they get to a miserable state they can change careers—just like Jackie Cooper did.

I am a firm believer in being happy. I was brought up to believe you could never get divorced. Yes, there was a time when people believed that to be true. But when I was watching my bride walk down the aisle to become my wife I reminded myself if this didn't work out I could get a divorce. I have never once wanted to exercise that option but I liked knowing I had that escape clause in my mind.

Forever is a long time and we should make as many decisions as we can to be happy. It may not have happened to you yet, but one day you are going to ask yourself or someone is going to ask you what are you doing the rest of your life? The answer is I am going to be happy and make as many people as I can around me happy.

## *My Buddy*

When I first arrived at Erskine College to start my college career, I was scared to death. Oh, I looked like I was full of confidence, but believe me I wasn't. I had a roommate I had never met, and a campus full of people who didn't know me. I was away from home and on my own.

One of the first people I met was Alph H. "Buddy" Browne. He was from Miami and had a car. Both of these facts impressed me. It made him appear to me to be rich, and I later learned he did come from a well-off family. His father was an oil company executive.

Buddy and I developed a friendship. We double dated a lot, studied together, and sat up some nights talking about life and such. I will not say Buddy was my best friend in college, but he was a good friend. I even went home with him to Miami at spring break one year. We went up to Fort Lauderdale and, yes, that was where the girls were.

Buddy was one of the best-natured people I ever knew. He took a lot of teasing from me and some of our friends. We were a sarcastic group who thought cutting someone down was hilarious and more often than not Buddy was the brunt of our jabs. He never retaliated, just went on with his life and with our friendships like we hadn't said a thing to him.

During those days, I was intense. My moods were all over the place and I could get angry over the least slight. I was popular, but that was because people put up with my moodiness. When I was not in a bad mood, I was great fun. So maybe it evened out. But because I was so moody and intense, I thought Buddy was shallow. He never seemed to have a bad mood and always seemed to be on an even keel.

He wasn't the best student, but he pulled through all right. He just wasn't analytical. I analyzed everything, but he didn't. He accepted things as they were and never worried over why they were. He was just good old Buddy Browne.

After college we didn't stay in touch and I really didn't think about him that much. I heard that he had gone into the business world and was successful. That didn't surprise me. I heard he had gotten married and had some kids and I was happy to hear that. Buddy deserved the love and attention of a good woman.

Then a year ago I heard from an Erskine classmate who told me Buddy was sick. She sent me his e-mail address and I wrote to him. He answered telling me all about his illness and how there really wasn't anything the doctors could do to make him well. He asked about my family and all and then he added at the end for me not to worry because the fat lady had not yet sung.

We have e-mailed back and forth for the past few months. The last one I got from Buddy he said that he thought the fat lady had come into the room and was warming up. I got the picture. I know Buddy's family will let me know if something happens. When it does I won't be surprised. Buddy has prepared me for the end.

What does surprise me is the depth of Buddy Browne. My college friend who I thought was so shallow has faced his illness with a determination and resolve that John Wane couldn't have mustered. He has shown me there is dignity in a life well lived. He has shown me that courage is possible in the face of death. He has also shown me that Christianity and faith can bring you peace.

I am already grieving for my buddy, Buddy Browne. He was a good friend of mine in college. He is a good friend of mine today. I am glad I got to know the power of this man. He has had a good life he tells me, and now he is ready to face death with dignity. I am awed by his strength.

Two days after I wrote this, the fat lady sang softly and Buddy passed into heaven. He was a good man, a good friend, and my buddy.

## *The Art of Isolation via E-Mails*

For years I looked forward to the postman delivering my mail. I would wait at the door around the time he was expected and anticipate what may be coming that day. Later I got a post office box so I could get the mail at any time of the day. But then I learned the post office didn't put mail in the boxes but once a day—and that was a disappointment.

I liked the excitement of receiving mail, the not knowing of what to expect. And when I got personal letters I liked the look of the stationary and the different aspects of handwriting. There was an art to letter writing that I never mastered, but I know many who did and their letters were treasures.

Now we have entered into the age of e-mail. We get brief notes dashed off to convey information. They arrive at all hours of the day or night and generally announce themselves with the melodious tones of "You've Got Mail" We read them and discard them, or rarely save them. They are not written as an art form but are rather sent just to convey information.

We can hide behind e-mails just as we hide behind answer machines and call waiting. If we don't want to talk we don't have to. Just let the machine get it. Then if we want to answer we can or we can deny the machine ever gave us the information.

The problem with e-mails is they are sterile, even with all the initials and smiley faces. With a phone call, you can hear the tone and timbre of a person's voice. You can get inflection, emotional additives, and even the power of silences. You can't get that from a short e-mail message.

I have a friend who communicates totally with his children by e-mail. I don't know if he is too cheap to call or if he just prefers the convenience of it. When I ask the last time he heard from his daughter, he refers to an e-mail he got. That's not hearing from someone. That's getting a message.

In some ways we are getting more and more isolated in our lives. We are hiding behind machines and letting them sort out who we talk with and when. We no longer have to learn the tactful way of avoidance because our machines do it for us.

Don't you wonder if people in the future will even know how to write a personal letter? Will all correspondence be reduced to the brief, abbreviated text? Will we write in the message jargon rather than use creative English? And will isolation become a way of life rather than a rarity?

## *Dream Big*

Today I spent a couple of hours at a local high school as a part of career day. The kids I met with are sophomores and juniors, which is pretty young to be talking about careers, but it seems you need to know early on where you're going to college and what you are going to study.

When I was in the eleventh grade, my English teacher asked what I was going to study in college and on a whim I said law. Eight years later and I had gone to college and law school and passed the bar. I was locked into a career as a lawyer and that was not what I wanted to be. So getting kids to commit at an early age can be harmful to the rest of their lives.

When I spoke to the students today I told them to follow their passion and to study what really appealed to them. I also asked them what they would be if they could be anything in the world. One said a music producer, another said a food critic, another opted for being an actor, and on and on. These were their dreams and it thrilled me that they were dreaming big. I urged them to hold on to their dreams and think positively.

I always tell students that it took me twenty-something years to find out what I should be doing. I now spend my time reviewing movies, books, and DVDs as well as writing books about my life. That sounds simple enough, but it took me forever to get up enough nerve to try. Then I always add if they want to be a writer then use me as an example. If I can do it, they can do it.

As I looked at this group of students today, I remembered an article on "the dumber generation," which is what they called the younger generation of today. Well, I disagree with that analysis. I think kids are plenty smart today. I don't think they are challenged enough sometimes, and I also think in some instances we put too much pressure on them. There has to be a happy balance.

Too many of us today just want our children to be happy. In having this as our main goal we let our children get away with things we shouldn't excuse. We excuse slacking off when they should be studying. We excuse bad behavior because it can't be their fault, or so we think. Happiness is a great thing but some of our happiness comes from a job well done, and a career well developed.

I don't know all the answers, but I do know we should all dream big. We should aspire to the heights in the field we love and expect that hard work and energy will bring success. We should tell our children they are special and then help in any way to make that come true.

People who have great expectations in their lives are my kind of people. They are the people who know inside themselves they are special and they are the ones who dream big.

## *A Reviewer's Life*

For years I have been a film critic. I see three movies a week and I write my opinion for several newspapers, websites, and then I appear on TV once a week and spout off there, too. I say what I think and let the chips fall where they might. After all it is only my opinion which is no better or no worse than anyone else's. Occasionally it gets awkward as when I recently interviewed Will Ferrell just after I had seen his bomb "Semi Pro." All through that interview, I was praying he would not ask me what I thought.

Still for the most part, I can do my movie reviews with no thought as to what the actors think. Brad, Angelina, and I do not do lunch. It has been a while since Julia called, and I really just don't get George Clooney. So there is nothing personal to be worried about when I rave or rant about a movie.

But I also do book reviews and those can be a problem. The problem is I know a lot of authors and consider some authors to be really good friends of mine. In many cases I review their efforts and in some cases I like what they have done and in others I do not. Believe it or not I say what I think. If I didn't what good would the review be?

Can that be awkward? Absolutely. There was a book I reviewed several months ago and I had looked forward to reading it because I knew the other works by this woman. I liked everything I had read and the information about the new book made it sound interesting.

As I was reading it, I thought, *Uh-oh, I am in trouble.* I absolutely did not like it and when I wrote my review I said so. Again it is just my opinion and nothing more. My comments were not going to make or break this lady's career. It has been awkward when I have seen this person since then. We never mention the review.

Another problem is I like to review my friends' books. I am a firm believer in publicity being the root of success in the publishing world. Now you have to have a good product but after that you have to get the word out about your book. Reviews and publicity are crucial so I like to get my friends' titles out there whenever possible.

I have been to a lot of festivals, writing courses, and other assemblies of authors and fans and have gotten to know a lot of writers. And most of the writers I have gotten to know, I have liked. From my reviews, I have started correspondence with many national writers. We e-mail back and forth and act like friends. From this I have begun to anticipate the next Jeffery Deaver novel, or the newest from John Lescroart, Jodi Picoult, Harlan Coben, etc. I have to make an actual concentrated effort to pick up books by new authors.

Finally there is the problem of the self-published author. My newspapers do not want a review of a self-published book and neither does my TV station. I am sorry it is like that but it is. I get copies of self-published books every week and I hate to set them aside, but it is the way things are.

I love to read. I love good writing. I love seeing talent shine. If I ever review one of your books please remember I am only being honest—and it is only one man's opinion.

## *Where Is the Cavalry?*

When I was growing up I watched John Wayne movies constantly. I liked the way he always won the day. No matter what the odds, he always came out on top. In other Westerns where the hero was not as successful as John Wayne, the United States Cavalry always rode to the rescue. The pioneers would be surrounded and about to be wiped out; then you would hear the bugle playing and the cavalry would ride in just in the nick of time.

That was then and this is now. The two most honored movies of last year were *No Country for Old Men* and *There Will Be Blood*. In both the bad guys apparently win. Javier Bardem's character Anton Chigurh is one of the most monstrous and despicable human beings ever depicted on screen. He kills without thought and without remorse. No cavalry rides to the rescue.

In *There Will Be Blood*, Daniel Day-Lewis brilliantly portrays Daniel Plainview, a man who does anything to succeed in business. At the end of the film, he even commits cold-blooded murder. Again no Cavalry stops his relentless attack on his victim.

Is this what Hollywood thinks we want? Or have they arbitrarily decided on no more heroes or happy endings? Neither *No Country* nor *Blood* broke any records at the box office. Even Oscar wins for Day-Lewis and Bardem couldn't entice people to pay to see such depressing films.

I turned to reading a good book to escape this negativism. I picked up John Grisham's latest, *The Appeal*. Grisham has gotten a little off the beaten path lately with his short books about romance and baseball, or his true-crime story, but this new book was supposed to be a return to the glory days of *A Time to Kill* or *The Rainmaker*.

The new book concerns an effort by big money to buy a Supreme Court judge in Mississippi. The owner of a huge corporation that has polluted land and water in Mississippi now wants to avoid the fines levied against him. I got into the story looking forward to the pages where the bad guy would get what was coming to him. Never happened. Even the great John Grisham let me down.

It seems the arts are entering into a period of pessimism. Gasoline prices are just going to continue to go up, the war in Iraq is never going to end, jobs are going to become more and more scarce, and the American dream is going to become a nightmare. We see it and we expect more of the same.

Not me. I am not going to give into this malaise. Negative thought begets negative happenings. I am going to go with the positive. I am going to believe in a brighter future. I am going to believe in the American Dream. I am going to listen for the sound of that bugle and wait for the cavalry to ride in and save the day.

## *Rumors of My Death*

Rumors have a way of taking on a life of their own. This was proven to me recently by some "rumors" I heard about one of my best friends. There are four or five of us who meet and eat lunch two or three times a week. Last week I dropped by on Friday. When I got to our usual table none of my friends were there. I asked our regular waitress if any of them had been in earlier. She said they hadn't but then she added, "But is it true the Judge had bypass surgery?"

I almost choked. This is a guy who I have known for years. My wife and I get together periodically with him and his wife to eat dinner and play catch up. This is also a man who is compulsively private. You don't get anything personal out of him unless you pry it out. He has been known to have medical tests run without me or his wife being aware of it. So was it possible he had had bypass surgery without me knowing it? Oh, yes.

I questioned the waitress a couple of more times about it and she assured me that was the information they had gotten. I also talked with the assistant manager of the restaurant who confirmed he had had three bypasses. She even told me who had told her and other details.

As soon as I left the restaurant and got into my car, I started making calls. I called the judge's house and got an answering machine. I left a message for his wife to call me and give me details about his surgery. Then I called the court where his office is. I left another frantic message there.

A few minutes later, his secretary called and asked me what in the world I was talking about. She said the judge was in St. Augustine, Florida, at a conference. She then added that a lawyer in town had had some bypasses and that must have been where the mixup occurred. Relieved by the news, I realized I had to call back to his house. I could just imagine what his wife would think when she heard my message. She still wasn't home so I left a second message telling her to ignore the first.

Later that night I did get her on the phone. She actually asked me if I thought the judge had told her he was going to St. Augustine but was in the hospital. I told her when he called that night to ask him to describe his day. She said she was going to get him to describe his room. I said to ask what kind of paintings were on the wall. She said she was going to ask if there were any crosses.

The next morning the judge called me on his way back from St. Augustine. He had talked to his wife and thought the whole thing was hilarious. I told him that had it been true he wouldn't have had to worry about dying because I would have killed him for not letting me know. Then I added that embarrassingly enough the first thought that had crossed my mind was "How long does it take to get over bypass surgery?" He and I are supposed to go to Biloxi in April and I didn't want to miss the trip.

He replied that he couldn't wait to go to lunch next week and amaze the people with how well and quickly he had recovered. He has a sense of the dramatic about him and I am sure he will play it all up to a fare thee well.

The judge can laugh about it and I can too, but there is a danger to spreading information that we aren't absolutely sure of, from a source that may or may not know of what he speaks. I know I can learn a lesson from this misinformation for I have been known to say, "Rumor has it..."

## *Talent Scouts*

Every time I sit down and watch *American Idol*, I think what a wonderful time it is to be alive and get to see such amazing talent in its early stages. Whatever you think of the show, it does offer a chance for anyone to be seen by millions of people. Before *American Idol*, your chances of being discovered as a talented singer were about ten thousand to one. Now thanks to *American Idol,* those odds have been pared down to a believable number.

People love to say that *American Idol* has run its course, but I certainly hope that's not true. Of course at some time Randy, Paula, and Simon are going to have to hang up their judges' robes. And maybe even Ryan Seacrest will have to step aside for a younger version, for there will always be people who can and will replace them.

The reason I hope the show goes on forever is that I think out there in the heartlands of America there is a child playing an air guitar or holding up a hairbrush and singing away to his/her hearts content. And while they are singing they are thinking about *American Idol* and knowing if they are good enough they too will get a chance to be seen and be heard.

It doesn't matter if they are from Atlanta or Perry, Georgia; from Hollywood or Redlands, California; big town or small town. It doesn't matter. The ticket is your talent if the *American Idol* train stops in a reachable city to let you hop on board.

Talent shows have been around forever. They probably held them in the Coliseum. Of course then if you didn't sing so pretty they would toss you to the lions. In some of our lifetimes, it was *Arthur Godfrey's Talent Scouts*. If my childhood memories serve me well, on that show a person would nominate another person to be on the show.

Then the nominated person would perform and people would write in their votes.

Later came *The Gong Show*, which was a talent show of sorts. If you weren't good you got gonged (and a lot of people were gonged). Still, every once in a while, you got a person who was actually talented.

More recently there was *Star Search*, which did discover some talented people. Yet somehow that show never had the impact *American Idol* has had. I never felt as if you got to know the people as completely on that show as you do on this new one. Today you become vested in the *American Idol* kids, especially the top ten winners.

America is known as the land of opportunity and a show like *American Idol* proves that to be true. It doesn't matter how rich you are, what color you are, who your parents are, or anything like that. If you can sing you have a chance.

So you kids out there watching *American Idol* start developing your dream. Know that one day you could be the next Carrie Underwood or Fantasia Barrino. Even if you don't win the title, you can still be a star like Daughtry or Clay Aiken.

This is the right time for anyone who is a singer to believe their dreams can come true. And that's one of the things that makes this country great and makes life worth living. Hope and opportunity—we couldn't ask for more.

## *Father of a Preacher Man*

There are things that lift you to the heavens and others that bring you to your knees. Then there are some things that do both. This is what happened when I went to church and listened to my son Sean preach. Now I have heard my son speak in church before, but that was when he was speaking as a youth minister. Today, he was speaking as a preacher on a Sunday morning.

Before he preached, he was nervous, and so was I. It isn't that I didn't have confidence in his abilities. I know how talented he is. Plus I knew God would take care of him. Still I wanted everything to go great for him so I was praying hard and often.

From his opening words, I knew he was going to reach the congregation. And when he removed his jacket in order to preach I knew they were going to relate to him. He spoke without notes and he was quoting scripture right and left. That seminary training really paid off.

As he spoke, I couldn't keep my mind from going back over the different phases of his life. Sean was born a "golden boy." He had blonde hair from birth and bright blue eyes. He was also the sweetest kid you could ever want to know. He just exuded love and I remember he would grab your leg and just hug you for no reason other than the fact you were there.

He was a small child until the summer before the tenth grade. Then he exploded and grew. The football coaches at his high school had largely ignored him, but now they came calling. Heck, they came begging. So he went out for the team and made it in the eleventh grade.

Sean was a good football player, but he would knock you down and then help you up. He had great enthusiasm and great team spirit and was the one who encouraged all the other players on the team. He loved the camaraderie of team sports and the just hanging out with the guys.

When he went to college, he joined a fraternity. That surprised us all because his brother had always told him fraternity brothers were only the best friends money could buy. Sean loved it even though he was not a drinker. His "brothers" called him "preacher" and he was the designated driver.

Sean always knew he wanted to be a youth minister. He worked at churches before, during, and after he attended college. Then he attended Asbury College in Kentucky and worked there too.

He has always been the type of child and adult you have to pinch yourself to make sure you aren't dreaming him. Not that he is perfect, but he isn't bad either. He is someone I would want to be friends with even if he wasn't my son.

Today was a momentous day. I was so proud I could have burst. I have been called many things in my life but "father of a preacher man" might be the best appellation yet.

## *Like Father, Like Son, Etc.*

It amazes me the things families have in common. I mean, there are so many traits we share unconsciously. One came to my attention recently when the family gathered together to celebrate the sixth birthday of my grandson Walker.

Walker is a gregarious, charming, fun-loving little boy. He loves sports, toys, and his sister. He is always in a good mood and rarely gets upset. What he doesn't like is the attention birthdays bring. Now don't get me wrong, he loves the presents; it's just the cake and the singing and all that stuff he'd rather do without.

In that way, he is like both me and his dad. I have never liked holidays or special occasions of any sort. I prefer the ordinary, routine days. The same is true of my son Sean. He would rather just skip all that holiday and celebratory stuff, especially that which brings attention to him. Sean and I have always laughed about how much alike we are in this area—and now we realize there is another member of the group and that's Walker.

These shared traits also involve food. I was talking with my brother this week and he was telling me how much he loves barbequed chicken wings, or hot wings as he calls them. He likes to dunk them in ranch dressing. That really sounds yucky to me but to each his own. Then when we were celebrating Walker's birthday at a local restaurant, Sean asked if he could order an appetizer and I said sure. He ordered hot wings with ranch dressing. I guess the hot wings gene jumped from my brother's side of the family to him.

When Sean was preaching at a local church a few weeks ago, when the service was over a friend of mine told me he was the best of Terry and me. What a great thing to hear, and I do hope it is true. Sean does have my outgoing personality. I can see that. He also has

Terry's sweet disposition, which is much better than mine will ever be.

Then there is my granddaughter Genna. When she was a few years old, my wife was told she was not a doll person. My wife definitely is. She loves to play dolls with small children. It is one of the ways she relates to them. When Genna comes to our house, she always asks for her doll. It is one my wife got for her and keeps at our house.

For her birthday this year, she asked for an American Girl doll and recently spent her own money to buy matching outfits for her and the doll. I guess she is a doll person now, and I think she inherited this from her Nana.

Life gives us a chance to see ourselves replicated over and over. When I look in the mirror now, I tend to see my father looking back. I didn't look that much like him as a younger man, but the older I get, the more I see him in me. It's weird.

We are all different and our own individuals, but inside us all there are also components we have inherited from the family tree. Good or bad, we are stuck with the traits of our ancestors and we are surely passing them on.

There are chips off the old block and apples that don't fall far from the tree. Let's just hope the traits we pass on are some of our best, but that choice isn't really ours to make.

## *Shout to the Lord*

My faith has been an important part of my life for many, many years now. Because of it, I am constantly on the lookout for Christian messages in entertainment. It is rare that I find it. In years gone by, stars such as Pat Boone made a big issue of their faith. He wouldn't kiss the girl in the movie and for that reason Shirley Jones remained unkissed in the film *April Love*.

I also grew up on epics such as *The Robe* and *The Big Fisherman*. *Ben-Hur* was another milestone religious film in my life. I even thought of *The Exorcist* as being a religious film. But as the years have gone by the examples of Christian teachings and Christian behavior in entertainment have become fewer and fewer.

After 9/11, there was a telethon in which Julia Roberts spoke. I don't remember if she made a speech or not, but I recall her saying simply "God is good." I was blown away. Now I know she is a Southern girl, but she is also an international star and coming out with a statement like that was an amazing witness to me.

Anyway, I was so amazed the other night when I was watching the "American Idol Gives Back" show. Everything about the show was touching my heart. It was more emotional than a Jerry Lewis telethon.

At the very end, the final eight contestants for *American Idol* were introduced. They came out dressed in white outfits and sang the Christian anthem "Shout to the Lord." It was a beautiful version of the song with David Cook doing a great job on his solo.

Then to my amazement, the next night they did the song again. And once more it was beautifully delivered. How in the world had they decided to sing the song? Who was the person who first suggested it and were all the idol contestants agreeable? Again, I don't know.

I do know that both versions have shown up on YouTube and over a half million people have watched the performances. That's staggering. I wonder how many people have downloaded it on to their iPods.

God works in wondrous ways and the presentation of that song may touch many, many people. I know it touched me. Now I also know there were some who might have been offended by it. I have seen comments on the Internet from people who objected to such an overtly Christian song. I can understand their comments and if some other type of religious song had been sung I might have been put off.

Still freedom of religion is just that—the right to put on a song with religious overtones or message. Our government wasn't doing it; the people at *American Idol* were. And I say more power to them.

"Shout to the Lord" made me want to shout Hallelujah!

## *A Weekend in the Country*

This past weekend my wife and I were invited to a wedding on Dafuskie Island, South Carolina. The idea of spending a couple of days on an island was immensely appealing to my wife. Not so much for me. Maybe it's some form of claustrophobia, but being stuck on an island with no way to get to the mainland except for a ferry that runs a few times a day rattles me.

I felt the same way when we went to Hawaii. I mean I was on an island in the middle of the Pacific Ocean. What if it sank! I can swim but not good enough or long enough to get back to the good old USA mainland. But at least in Hawaii you had grocery stores and movie theaters. On Dafuskie you basically have the basics and nature.

Communing with nature is not one of my things. If nature wants to commune with me it can come to my house and sit down and talk. My idea of enjoying wildlife is to have a wild time reading a book or seeing a movie. Bugs, reptiles, and other creatures are not my thing.

Anyway, I digress. We drove down to Hilton Head, South Carolina, on Saturday morning. The ferry was leaving at one. Mapquest said it would take us three hours and nineteen minutes to get there. By leaving at 8:30 in the morning I thought we would have more than enough time. And we did. But then we had to stop and buy me some socks. I had forgotten to pack any. And then we wanted to eat. We always want to eat.

I remembered a little restaurant I had eaten at on an earlier trip. The chili was just as good as I remembered it. I was enjoying it so much I didn't look at the time. When we came out of the restaurant I realized we had twenty minutes to go thirteen miles.

We didn't speed, but we went the maximum. Somehow we also managed to make every traffic light right. Still we pulled up at the ferry at 1:01. The baggage had already been loaded but they made a special run for us and we were able to get on the boat and get settled for the forty-five-minute ride. Fortunately, they were having some problems with the boats. They had been running late all day and some runs on the previous day had been cancelled.

We arrived at the hotel around 2:15. Our bags made it to our room, which is always a good thing, and that included the bag that had my Diet Cokes, cheese-and-peanut-butter crackers, and M&M's. I told you I don't "rough it."

I did panic when I realized I had left my fan at home. I always have a fan running at the side of our bed, so I just knew I was going to have a sleepless night. Turns out I was so tired by the time we made it to bed, I slept like a stone.

The wedding was beautiful. It was held outside despite fears the weather was not going to cooperate. We had ridden over on the ferry with the woman in charge of the reception (She spoke with a Jamaican accent and I told her I could listen to her talk all day long.) and I told her to save me a lot of food at the reception. I needn't have worried; there was enough food for an army. There was roast beef, shrimp and grits, grilled chicken, potatoes, vegetables, and much, much more. I didn't even have to rely on my crackers and Diet Cokes.

The rain held off all afternoon and night as we partied hearty. The bride and groom were picture perfect and seemed to be totally pleased with everything. There was even a rainbow in the sky as they were taking their vows.

The next day we left the island, took the ferry back to the mainland, lunched at an Italian restaurant, and got home in time for me to review a current movie. Now there's my idea of a wild life.

## *Can You Hear Me Now?*

It has been a while since I went on one of my rants, but circumstances this week have forced my hand. I was told that I could get a new phone through my cell phone supplier and it would be free. This was because I had had my contract for over two years. Since my cell phone is a little grungy from use I thought it might be a good idea to pick up a new one.

When I went to shop for a new phone, there were no customers at the counter so I walked right up. Not so fast, dodo, I had to go back and sign in and give my cell phone number to a machine. I also had to state the purpose of my visit. After that was done, I waited (though there were no other customers) and eventually my name was called.

I stated I had come for my free phone. The girl, who looked terminally bored, asked for my password. I told her to give me a clue and she settled for the last four digits of my social security number.

When I asked if the phone would be free, she replied I would have to sign up for another two year contract. I said fine. She then showed me what my "free" phone would look like. I commented it looked pretty good for a free phone. That's when she said there would be a twenty dollar activation fee. I asked her why there would be an activation fee when I was already active in her system. She said that was the way it was.

I asked if that meant I had to pay twenty dollars and sign up for another two years too. She said yes. I asked if I would still get a phone with my same number and the information in my current phone transferred to it. She said yes, but there would be a ten dollar transfer fee. Since it only means taking a chip out of one phone and putting it in another, I asked what the fee was for. She said that's the way it is.

So it turned out my "free phone" would cost me twenty dollars for activation, a two year extension on my contract that requires a fee if I drop the service earlier than two years, and a ten dollar transfer fee. All because that's the way it is.

By this time, I was foaming at the mouth. I am just so sick of being preyed upon as a customer rather than being valued. It seems businesses are out to get you any way they can. Not only are they bored waiting on you, they don't want to provide you with any incentive to be their customer. That's just the way it is.

So having heard all this from the bored out of her mind representative I told her she could forget it and I would keep my phone. It barely registered on her mind as she looked to see who was next on the list.

Sometimes you want to do something just to make yourself feel better and writing this all down has served that purpose.

Hey, cell phone company, can you hear me now?

## *Just Lock Me in the Car Again*

Last week my son Sean was preaching at a church in Perry. He went to the church early and my wife, daughter-in-law, two grandchildren, and I came later. We arrived at the church and were getting out of my daughter-in-law Paula's car. She, my granddaughter Genna, my wife Terry, and I got out, but somehow my grandson Walker got locked inside.

I hollered to Paula that Walker was locked in the car and I couldn't get the door open. She unlocked the car with her key fob. When Walker exited the car, he had his Gameboy in his hands. Paula saw it and told him he could not take it into church with him. Looking totally forlorn, he told her just to lock him in the car again.

Don't you sometimes feel that way too? On those days when the lawn needs mowing, too many bills are due, the air conditioners on the blink, don't you just want somebody to lock you in the car and leave you alone? I know I do. I could completely empathize with what Walker was saying.

Take the other night. I was driving back from Moultrie, Georgia, where I had been for a book signing. I came over a hill and there in the middle of the road was part of a truck tire. I hit that sucker going seventy miles an hour and it made a lot of noise.

I immediately began my God-don't-let-me-down prayer. *Just let me get home*, I prayed, and sure enough I did. I said my thanks and went in the house and went to bed. My wife woke me the next morning with the announcement that something had leaked out from my car and was covering the driveway.

It was transmission fluid and it was everywhere. All I could think was that somebody could just lock me in the car and leave me alone and I would be happy. I wouldn't get out and I wouldn't let anyone get in.

But life isn't that way. I got back in my car, cranked it up, and begin my next prayer: *God, please get me to the garage.* The garage is about ten blocks away and I honestly didn't think the car would go one block, much less ten. But, sure enough, I made it all the way there.

When my friend Thomas, who works there, brought me back to my house, he looked at the driveway and said he couldn't believe I made it home, much less to the garage. I told him that when I woke up and saw the liquid everywhere I just wanted someone to lock me in my car and leave me alone. He said he knew what I meant since he had had days like that too.

Yes, I guess we have all had days like that. But just remember you always have to get out of the car eventually. And when you do things generally work out alright. You may not be able to take your Gameboy into church, but most other things have a way of straightening themselves out.

## *Exercise Will Kill You*

Rarely does a day go by that some idiot doesn't ask me about my exercise regimen. When I tell them I don't have one, they act shocked. Then they try to rephrase the question so they can get a good answer, and all they get is the same answer. I don't exercise. I am a sloth. I don't really like the outdoors.

Today my brother told me about going to his exercise class. He has had knee replacement surgery and the doctors want him to exercise. I have both my original knees, thank you very much. They haven't worn out because I have protected them.

My brother asked me how long I could stand balanced on one leg with my eyes closed. I told him I didn't have a clue and asked why would I want to know that. He responded that they did it in his exercise class and it shows how much balance you have. I told him I had enough balance to walk upright and not topple over, and that's all I need to know.

This lack of exercise thing is not something new. I have felt this way for most of my life. I remember when that famous runner collapsed and died at an early age. I pointed to his story as exhibit A and told all my friends what has become my mantra: exercise can kill you.

When I was in the Air Force, I went to officer training school. One of the requirements was we had to run a mile. It was the worst part of my training as I don't like to run anywhere. I remember our commanding officer screaming at me, "Run, Jackie, run." I put everything I had into making that mile and slowly collapsed in front of him. He told me to stand up and shake it off. I stood up and promptly threw up all over him. I guess he was the one who had to shake it off.

Now don't get me wrong. I want to be healthy and live a long life. I know I am overweight and need to shed a few pounds, but I would rather do it through diet rather than exercise. I would really rather do it through diet pills, but my doctor won't prescribe them for me.

Several years ago, I had a doctor who would. I took those little tablets and my metabolism flew into overdrive. I am hyper by nature and I was superhyper on those pills. And I lost weight. Man, did I lose weight. I could almost sit back and watch it drop off. But I was also bouncing off the walls, so I had to give up the pills. Within a few weeks, I had gained back all the pounds I had lost and some brought along friends.

When I was a teenager, my parents worried about me because I was so skinny. I stayed that way until I was in my early twenties. Then it was like somebody added water and I became the Pillsbury Doughboy. Don't ask me to explain it—it just happened.

So if you run into me on the street avoid the subject of exercise. I get a little testy when it is mentioned. Remember, exercise can kill you.

## *Try a Little Harder, Be a Little Better*

This week I got the news that my son Sean has been selected as pastor for a church in Perry. Sean and his family had already planned to move back to Perry, but this let's them know they're making the right move. My daughter-in-law will be teaching and my son Sean will be preaching. As for me, I will be trying to be a better person.

Now Sean has been a youth minister for several years, but this is his first job as a full-fledged pastor of a congregation. Also, he's always served in cities other than Perry. In other words, I have not had to feel the heat of being a preacher's dad, but boy am I feeling it now.

I have always heard how difficult it is to be a preacher's kid. I had friends who had a parent who was a preacher when I was growing up. They told me they always felt like they were on display and were being judged. They said the least infraction could get blown up just because of the fact their father was a preacher.

Now I am in that club with the preacher's kids, but I am the parent of a preacher. In truth it is the same thing. I want to set an example because of who my son is. I don't want anyone to be able to criticize him because of who I am and what I do. With me being a movie critic, there may be some who think I am not setting the best example.

I remember clearly when we lived in California both of my boys were playing soccer. I was watching one of their games and this woman came up and began to talk with me. She also had a son on the team. She asked me if I was the one who wrote movie reviews for the local newspaper. I answered that I was. Then she said that she was surprised because she had heard I was a Christian.

I told her I was a Christian and she said she didn't think I could be and see the movies I saw. So, you see what I am up against. I tried to explain to that lady that I review movies in order to let people know what is contained in them. Then they can decide if they or their families should watch them or not. She didn't seem to accept that as justification.

Sean has never asked me to change my job in order to take the pressure off of him. He doesn't see a conflict between reviewing movies and being a Christian. And as long as he doesn't mind, I will continue to do it.

I will also pray harder to be a better person. We are all sinners in one sense or another, but we can all try to be better examples. That's what I am going to do. I am going to try a little harder to be a little better. I won't be making gigantic changes overnight but with one small step at a time I hope I get there.

It's going to be a different world being the father of the pastor at the church I attend, but it is also going to be one of the richest blessings anyone can receive. I can't wait for June 15 to get here and for my son to start preaching his sermons and serving his flock.

## *The Way We Read*

I am sure there are people out there who can gauge our personalities by how we read and what we read. I don't have the knowledge to do that kind of thing, but I do know we humans vary in the way we do these things and what we choose. Over the years, I have observed the variety of ways our reading habits form.

For example, I am a first word, first sentence, first chapter type of person. I start at the beginning and head on with no looking back. If the book is really good I like to read it in one sitting, if possible. If it only mildly entertains me, I put it aside, pick it up and read a little, and slowly but surely make my way through it. I rarely stop reading a book once I start.

My brother has a different way of reading. He reads two or three books at a time. He will read a chapter in one and then move on to the other(s). He never cheats and reads more than one chapter at a time no matter how exciting or compelling the book is. He has done this since grammar school, so I guess it is totally ingrained in him now.

He also has a stack of books that he is considering reading. He never moves a new book to the head of his stack or list. Each must wait its turn. There is no cheating allowed. Even when I wrote my first book, it went into the stack and had to wait its turn before he read it.

Then there is my favorite quirky reader. I have a friend who always reads the last chapter of any book she is considering. If the last chapter interests her, then she reads the entire book from the front. I have asked her if finding out "who done it" ruins it for her, and she always says no.

This process is better than another friend's. He skims the entire book before he reads it. After he skims, it he reads it for the details.

Why not just read it cover to cover? His answer is he has always done it this way. If it works for him...

My friends also have a variety of book types they like. One never reads anything but always just listens to them on tape. I have to admit I have not come under the spell of the books-on-tape craze. I can't think of any person whose reading would so entrance me that I would want to hear a whole book on tape. I prefer to read the words and let my imagination provide the looks and sounds of the characters.

Another friend only reads non-fiction. She says she wouldn't waste her time reading a made-up story. She is balanced by another friend of mine who only reads fiction. She says she has no desire to read non-fiction stories. I just couldn't be that rigid. I take my reading pleasure where I find it.

A publicist for one of the major book publishers e-mailed me the other day. She said she would put me on her list for review copies of books. She then asked me what type of books I preferred. I pondered over that and then replied, "Good books!" I just don't have a special category. I am willing to try anything from science fiction to historical non-fiction. I guess I prefer fiction, but I am open.

Like those individual snowflakes, we all have our reading peculiarities and none of us are exactly alike. I, for one, am very pleased it is that way.

Happy reading!

## *Walking Tall*

Okay, I have to admit it. I have started walking. Well, I've been walking since infancy, but now I have joined the ranks of those people who walk for their health. I fought the good fight, but now I have decided to give up and join them.

My wife is in a state of shock. She has been walking for ages, but when she tried to get me to join her I stayed in bed. I always reminded her to take her keys, good husband that I am. Then off she would go and I would get back to sleeping.

Maybe it was Tim Russert's death that made me change my mind. I saw a doctor on television discussing Russert's untimely death and he stated your waist should be no more than half your height. By those calculations, I should be eight feet tall, and I'm not. I wish I could solve my health problems by growing taller and not have to shrink my waist, but I think my growth spurts are at an end.

When I was a teenager, I was a stick. I just didn't gain weight. Whatever my metabolism was then it made me thin. So why don't we keep that same metabolism all of our life! Mine changed sometime around my last year in law school. Up till then, I could eat anything I wanted and not gain an ounce. I didn't do a lot of physical activity then either, but it didn't matter. I was a lean, mean fighting machine. Well, at least I was lean.

When my metabolism changed, it changed over night. Honestly it did. I have stretch marks from how I ballooned up so fast. I had to buy a whole new wardrobe of clothes because everything became tight at one time. Only my socks still fit.

From that point on, I've battled with my weight. I can now look at food and gain a few pounds. And when I eat, well, Katie, bar the door. Those pounds come rushing to me like they are having a picnic. My pounds love me and fight to stay with me.

But now I am part of the walking elite. I get out there every morning and walk at least a couple of miles. It almost kills me, but I am determined to keep doing it. One thing that helps is counting my steps. I keep a cadence of sorts on my left foot and count each stride.

Maybe the counting keeps my mind occupied, but whatever the reason I can make the distance if I count it off. I don't talk to anyone. I don't listen to music. I just put my head down and count off the steps. My head only pops up when I hear a car approaching.

Hopefully walking will decrease my waist size. I really would hate to think I have got to grow taller in order to survive, but if I must I must.

## *The Write Stuff*

In a few days, I will be taking part in something new and novel titled the Georgia Authors Book Bash. It will be held at the Margaret Mitchell House in Atlanta and will feature sixty authors, mainly from Georgia but also some adjoining states. For a fee, the public can come in and mingle with the authors, buy their books, get them signed, and ask questions.

I love events like this. Writers have become the rock stars of the new millennium and people are clamoring to meet and greet them. This event will feature such luminaries as Joshilyn Jackson, Ferrol Sams, Brian Jay Corrigan, Emily Giffin, David Bottoms, and a ton more. If you want to learn more about the literary scene in Georgia, this is the place to do it.

This is also a time for aspiring writers to come out and talk with people who have made it so to speak. I always tell people if I could do it, you can do it. When you get a chance to meet some of these superstars, I think you will find they say the same thing. The world of writers is not some exclusive club. There are no secret handshakes, no required secret words. It is open to everyone.

Since I have started meeting more and more authors I have found them to be the nicest people you would ever want to meet. I went to a picnic last weekend sponsored by the Atlanta Writers Club. This group was presenting an award to Terry Kay. I am a huge Terry Kay fan so I wanted to be there to offer my congratulations. Long story short, I got there late and missed the presentation, but I did get to visit with Terry and also with two other writer friends, Milam Propst and Augusta Trobaugh. Milam is the author of several books, but her most well known is *A Flower Blooms on Charlotte Street*. This story about her grandmother was made into the very popular family film *The Adventures of Ociee Nash*.

At the picnic, Milam and I discussed the fact she is working on a new book and it is another Ociee Nash story. How great is that! Milam is working with Belle Books and the great Deb Smith, so we have this new "adventure" to anticipate. Milam will also be at the Georgia Authors Book Bash on Sunday.

Augusta Trobaugh wrote one of my favorite books, *Sophie and the Rising Son*. She was telling me it has been optioned as a movie but added that you can't count on something like that until it actually happens. Still I would love to see a movie version of this great story.

Terry Kay is a friend to Augusta, Milam, and me. In fact he is a friend to all writers in Georgia and around the country. That was the basis for the award he received. If you ever want a word of encouragement, go to Terry. If you ever want your spirits lifted, go to Terry. If you ever want to be inspired, go to Terry.

He is recognized as one of the very best writers Georgia has ever produced. If you want proof of this, read his latest novel *The Book of Marie*. It is Terry Kay at his best. He pours his heart into his writing and the result is a book that touches your heart.

The world of books is a place where you can enter other worlds, have amazing experiences, and through the authors meet some of the most talented people on the face of the earth. I stand in awe of those I know who write, and do it successfully.

## *Beat the Clock*

Years and years ago there was a show on television called *Beat the Clock*. Contestants had to complete certain tasks before the clock ran out. They would run races or do other stunts and all the while the clock ticked ominously.

Some days I feel I am a contestant on *Beat the Clock*. I don't know how old I was when I realized that life is finite, but that's when the countdown began. I realized I only had a limited amount of time to accomplish my goals. Sure obstacles could arise to prevent me from doing these things such as illness, injury, etc., I starting racing to live my life. In fact, I always feel like I have to be doing something, have to be accomplishing something. That's why I am so miserable on vacations. I don't like dead time.

My wife and I had a discussion about this. She likes having time to de-stress and chill out. To me that's like dog paddling in the ocean. If you are going to swim, swim! I don't like idle time. I like to have goals to accomplish and things to do. That's why I am a list maker. I write down things I have to do and then check them off as I get them done. Now some people make lists of things for other people to do. Not me, I just make my own list. I have to beat the clock.

What brought this to mind was my son asking me the other day when I was going to write my novel. I have said I was going to write a book about my life, but it had to wait until after my stepmother died. It will be a fictional account, but it will deal with the problems I encountered growing up. I have been talking about this forever, but he reminded me my stepmother has died and I should get started on it.

He then asked me how long it would take me to write it and I answered quickly that it would probably take years and years. He looked at me like I was crazy and then added that I had better get started. And I guess I had.

It doesn't matter if you are ten, twenty, thirty, forty, or older—you are in a race against the clock if you have things you want to accomplish. Life is finite and the end could come at any time. That's not being fatalistic; that's being realistic.

I am a planner and I have things I have planned to accomplish. Of course, I keep revising my list and adding to it. I think that's what keeps life interesting and fun. I will still go on vacations from time to time as my family seems to enjoy them, but for me the fun of life is in the race. I just hope my clock runs for many, many more years.

## *Lonely Hearts*

My wife has been in St. Petersburg, Florida this past week visiting her mother. She went because her mother wasn't feeling well, but then spent a few extra days just to be with her. Since Terry's dad died last year, she tries to go visit her mother as often as she can. After her husband's death, my mother-in-law is struggling with loneliness. She says no one knows what loneliness of this type is like until they go through it.

While Terry was gone, I got lonesome but it was nothing compared to what I know her mother is going through. I could always talk with Terry by phone and I always knew the separation had a limit. The loneliness Terry's mother is going through just goes on and on.

We have asked her mother to move up to Perry, but she doesn't want to leave her home. She says that any time she is away, the house "pulls" her back. I guess she is referring to the pull of memories, and I can understand that feeling.

After my mother died, I felt so lonesome for her that I didn't think I could stand it. There was a void in my heart, an emptiness I couldn't fill. I tried to explain to people how I felt but mere words couldn't do it. The closest I could come was to say I felt homesick for her.

Maybe that's the best way to describe loneliness. It is homesickness at its worst. There are places that our hearts call home, places where we can relax and be ourselves and feel completely loved and wanted. When we lose one of these places, we become homesick for it. We want it back.

I watched a video on YouTube the other day about two men and the lion cub they raised as a pet. When the lion grew up, it became too large to keep as a pet so the men took it to Africa and released it into the wild. A year or so later, they were so homesick for this lion, which they had named Christian, they contacted people in Africa and asked if anyone knew where Christian was.

They were told he had become the head of his own pride and that he was completely at home in the wild. They were told it would not be a good idea to try to find and see him as he was now a wild animal. But the heart knows what the heart knows and these two men went to Africa anyway and looked for the lion.

One day they found him and when he saw them he exploded with joy. I mean you can see it in the video of the meeting. The lion is overjoyed and jumps up on the two men and licks them and seems to embrace them. It is a reunion like you have never seen.

Is this a true story or is it a doctored video? I don't know. More importantly, I don't care. It is the essence of the film that I want to believe, and I do. I think the bond of love lives within us and when it is severed there is loneliness and homesickness. A rejoining of that bond is a cause for celebration.

We need to be more accessible to those we love. The only thing that fills a void of lost love is more love. If you can help someone just by loving them, then do it. There is nothing worse than being lonely, and there are way too many lonely people in our world today.

## *The Security of Sameness*

When I was growing up in Clinton, South Carolina, I went to school with the same people from kindergarten through my senior year. Jimmy, Myrna, Julia, Wallace, Lou Jones, John, and about thirty more kids were with me from beginning to end. Traditionally, very few people moved to Clinton and very few moved away.

The upshot of this was I never had to worry about being around strangers. No matter who I got assigned as my new teacher, I always knew I would be with familiar people in the class. I could look to my right and look to my left and there were familiar faces.

Even when I graduated and went to college, I went with about fifteen of my Clinton High classmates. So though I met a bunch of new people when I entered Erskine College, I also knew a good segment of the freshman class. And when I went to law school three of my closest friends went to graduate school in Columbia, South Carolina, and we all shared an apartment.

There is something to be said about sameness. Seeing familiar faces can be comforting and provide security. I thought about this recently because this is the first week of school for my grandchildren. Walker is going into the first grade and Genna is going into third. Walker is going to the school where his mother teaches and Genna is going to the school where her Nana is director.

Before school started Terry, my wife, was able to arrange a play date for Genna with some of the girls who would be in her class. Genna really took to the girls and this week she didn't walk into a class of strangers. She said her first day at school was wonderful.

Because they had just moved back to Perry, Paula didn't know who would be in Walker's class. When he came home from his first day he complained he didn't know anybody. He acted like they would all stay strangers to him forever, but knowing Walker they won't. He has his daddy's personality and they will all be his best friends by week's end.

Being around people we know whether it be in school, church, work or in our neighborhoods makes a difference. Knowing each other adds to our security. We know who we can rely on if we need a friend. We know who to call when we have trouble. We know who will watch our homes and watch our backs.

I grew up in a place of familiar faces, and that's one of the main reasons I have always loved my adopted town of Perry, Georgia. It quickly became a place of familiar faces. When I go to church, I see people I know. When I go to the grocery store, I see people I know. When I go to the post office, I see people I know. And it is always a good feeling.

Surround yourself with friends if you can. Do not live an isolated life. We all need people whether we want to admit it or not. We need them for warmth, happiness, and for security.

## *The Dahlonega Literary Festival*

This past weekend I participated in the Dahlonega Literary Festival in Dahlonega, Georgia. Dahlonega is a town about fifty miles above Atlanta in North Georgia. Last year, the festival was held in February and it was *cold*! This year the weather was just right.

Dahlonega is a town with a lot of flavor. It has a great town square with a variety of quaint shops. Some of these shops were used as the venues for readings during the festival. Most events however took place in the community house a block or so off the square.

Among the authors participating in the events were Steve Berry, Patti Callahan Henry, Joshilyn Jackson, Karen Abbott, Nathalie Dupree, Jack Bass, William Rawlings, Jackie Miles, Julie Cannon, Patricia Sprinkle, Karen White, and Cathy Kaemmerlin. Others were there but these are the ones I got to spend the most time with.

Steve Berry is from St. Mary's right outside of Savannah. I have been reading everything Steve writes since I read *The Amber Room*. It was so interesting to learn about Steve's career and his meteoric rise as a writer of thrillers. His fans are legion and they all wait hungrily for his next work to arrive.

The same is true of Patti Callahan Henry. She writes novels that touch the heart and challenge the brain. Excitingly, Patti's parents were in attendance. George and Bonnie Callahan are two of the nicest people you would ever want to meet. I am crazy about Patti but having these two along was icing on the cake.

The team behind the festival made sure we were all treated royally. They arranged a room for me at a local bed and breakfast and it was charming. It is called the Worley Homestead Bed and Breakfast and Francis Mauldin, who owns it with her husband Bill, even provided me with a little electric fan for my room. I couldn't have asked for more.

One of the surprising things I learned about the Dahlonega area is that there are several winery's there. Now, I'm no wine connoisseur but the local wine was smooth and delicious. Plus the views I found overlooking the vineyards were breathtaking. I thought I had been transported to the Napa Valley in California.

The town, the people, the accommodations, the authors, the landscape, the weather—everything came together to make this one of the most enjoyable festivals I have attended in some time. The people who put this festival together are to be commended for knowing how to do it right.

If you missed it, well, there's always next year. If you were there, then I hope you had as good a time as I did. It was three days of literary fun with as compatible a group of people as I have ever had the pleasure of meeting. Let's do it again next year!

## *My Friend Karen*

A few years ago, I was at a book event and met the one and only Karen Spears Zacharias. Karen had just written a book about her life growing up in Columbus, Georgia, called *Hero Mama*.

*Hero Mama* not only dealt with Karen's life but also described how her mother raised a family after Karen's father was killed in Vietnam. It's not a glossy picture of American family life but was rather a truthful one that shows warts and all. As I read it, I thought, *How can this woman be this truthful?* I also thought, *This woman's family is going to kill her!*

But that's Karen. She's honest to a fault. Plus she has very definite opinions and she lets them be known. Maybe that's why just recently she was hired as an op-ed writer for the *Fayetteville Observer* of North Carolina.

Karen is a fierce advocate for veterans rights as well as the rights of their families. She has campaigned tirelessly for better medical care and other issues. When Karen believes in you or a cause, then she believes all the way. Don't try to stand in her way when she is on a march for her beliefs or she will run you over.

Recently Karen wrote a new book titled *Where's Your Jesus Now?* It deals with how various fears are eroding our faith. The book is pure Karen—open, honest, shocking, touching, challenging, and inspiring. Some may think it is too honest, but none will be able to doubt the sincerity of what she writes.

I liked this book for many reasons, but I liked it most for its humor. That's another trait Karen has. She sees the humor in life. One of the first things I noticed about her was her laugh. It is a solid laugh, not a titter, and it explodes from her when she's amused.

I don't get to see Karen as much as I would like. Usually we run into each other at a book festival here and there. Still we keep up with each other through e-mail and now Facebook. Yes, we are Facebook friends—whatever that means.

I urge you to pick up Karen's book no matter your religion. I gave copies to both my Sunday school teacher and my pastor, and also to some of my good friends. All have had positive responses to Karen's words. Most commented about how direct and open she is about life and the people she has encountered.

Karen is one of those people you don't forget no matter how little you see her. Once you have been bowled over by her you are never the same. She is a "hero mama" in her own right and a true friend to many, many people. She is fascinating and intriguing while at the same time easy to be around.

Life brings a variety of people into our lives. I am glad Karen came into mine. She is my good friend and I recommend her books to you.

## *Carry Me Back*

When my father died, I inherited two homes in Clinton, South Carolina. It was a complex inheritance as my stepmother got a life estate, and then upon her death they came to me. I got the "happy house" where I grew up, and the "other one" where I lived with my father and stepmother. These two houses represent the best and the worst times of my life.

When my stepmother died a few months ago, I went into the "happy house" for the first time in years. The feelings it engendered were still there, but the house itself was in terrible shape. One of the front windows was broken out, the ceilings were sagging, and the yard was in bad shape. Still if I closed my eyes a little, the memories could recreate the house as it had been.

My parents bought "the happy house" many years ago when I was still a very small child. We were already living on Holland Street. We rented rooms with Miss Bessie Adair who had a huge two-storey home. Later when my parents bought a couple of lots they bought them just a block away on Holland Street.

The house my parents built has two bedrooms, one bathroom, a kitchen, and a living room. None of the rooms was especially big but to us it was a mansion. The day we moved into the new house, it rained. That's the only thing I can remember about the actual move. Daddy had borrowed someone's truck and all the stuff in the back of the truck got soaked.

Even wet, we moved in on that day and spent the night in our new home. I remember that first night I could hear the rain on the roof and it gave me such a feeling of security. It was like I was cocooned in a place where no harm could ever come. And that feeling stayed with me for many years to come. I was happy in that house and I think my entire family was.

Of course, my life in that house ended badly when my mother discovered she had cancer. We were living there when she died. But even with that tragedy invading, I still loved that house. It was still the place of my security.

A few months after my mother died, my father decided to remarry. I was horrified and told him I could not bear for anyone else to live in my mother's house. He told me he planned to build a new house on the corner lot we owned. My Uncle Frank had agreed to build the house for him and his future wife.

The house wasn't finished until after the one year anniversary of my mother's death. After the wedding we moved into the new house. This new one never gave me any sense of security and my days there were not happy.

I am going to go back to Clinton in a few weeks and take a look at the two houses that dominated my childhood. I hope I make a ton of money off of that second house. I've already taken a loss with it for many years.

I am going back to Clinton in a few weeks and will look again at the houses' interiors. I am sure the "happy house" will still give me feelings of warmth and pleasure. That other house, well I hope we can sell it fast. It has already cost me more than just money. It cost me my teen years as it filled me with unhappiness and quiet desperation. Maybe the next family who lives there can eke out some happiness within its walls. I never could.

## *About Facebook*

A few weeks ago my friend Bobbie Eakes sent me an e-mail saying she wanted to be my friend on Facebook. I didn't have a clue as to what she was talking about but because I like Bobbie I clicked yes. This brought up a screen saying I needed to join Facebook in order to be Bobbie's friend. It was free and relatively simple so I did what was required. Lo and behold, I got my own page to which I added a picture and some identifying data.

I still didn't know what I was doing but soon I began to receive invitations to be friends with people. Some of these people I knew and some of them I didn't. But being a friendly sort of person I said yes to them all. Who doesn't want to be friends?

Since that time I have received invitations to join groups—I said yes. I have had people write on my wall (It took me a while to figure out what my wall was.). I have even received gifts, I think. Best of all is the way people update their happenings and let me know what they are doing.

Since I joined Facebook I have also received an invitation to join Linkedin. I joined it too. Why not? I am trying to get with this new age of web life. For so long, I knew how to send e-mail and that was it. Now I at least know how to Google.

I still haven't gotten into the texting thing and my cellphone is a relic from the days of yore. It doesn't do anything but ring and let me talk. I can't get my e-mail off it and I can't surf the web. My son has a phone that does everything but cook supper.

I'm trying to stay up to date but I'm fast falling behind. Technology is on a roll and if you aren't on board then just get out of the way. It seems that colleges are going to start requiring everyone to have a cell phone and possibly even a laptop. I have heard that in a few years, we won't have newspapers or even books.

If you don't like those ideas, well, too bad because the new tech is virtually going to be stuffed down our throats. One thing impending is the disappearance of check writing, which I am clinging to like the last leaves of summer. I like writing out the payments for my bills and then checking them off as the checks clear. I don't like just sending payments via the computer. It's so impersonal and hands-off.

It is too late in the game to do an about face, or more particularly an about Facebook. We have to get with the program. That's why I am a Facebook member. I am making progress one face at a time.

## *Tomorrow*

I have always been a person who enjoys anticipation. From my earliest years, I had to have something to look forward to happening. It might be something small or it might be something big, but I liked having something joyful happening in the future.

My concepts of enjoyment of life have changed some since those early days, but I know people who still look to tomorrow to bring happiness, and never concentrate on the todays. Just like Annie sang about the sun coming out tomorrow, some people live for the happiness of the future. The problem with that is overlooking the joys of today.

Fortunately, I think I'm living in that future I always anticipated. A lot of times when I was a pre-teen and even teenager I would say things that began, "When I grow up" or "When I am on my own." Well, I am there now.

When I entered the workforce, I talked about what I would do when I retired. Guess what? I am retired. Now I do just what I want to do and when I want to do it. There is no dreaming of what will happen in the future. The future is now.

One of the things I used to dream of was having a *Dallas*-like home. By that, I mean having one son and his family live in one wing of my house and the other son and his family living in the other. If it was good enough for Bobby and JR, it was good enough for me.

Well, I didn't end up with a *Dallas* living arrangement but I did get my youngest son and his family living in the same town with me. His kids are as comfortable and at ease in my house as they are in their own. I see them just about every day as we go to the same church, eat together a few times a week, and visit together at other times.

All my dreams have come true. I relish my past, enjoy my present and appreciate my future which I hope is more of the same. How fortunate can you be? It is like I designed it all and it just fell into place.

I am just glad I recognized that we sometimes reach our tomorrows. They don't always stay stuck in a future time warp. I would hate to have gone through the rest of my life dreaming of all those golden tomorrows and thereby missing all the wonders of today.

All of my days are golden time and it is in the present. The sun is out and shining and I don't have to be assured the sun will come out tomorrow. You can stop that song, Annie. Tomorrow is here.

## *Highs and Lows*

Some people are even-keeled all the time. They sail through life rolling with whatever comes their way. I am not that way. I am a man of highs and lows. The highs can be brought on by the most insignificant things and the lows can be triggered by the most commonplace occurrences. This past weekend was a good example.

First off, my birthday was on Saturday and anybody who knows me knows I don't like birthdays, holidays, etc. Still I have to say my wife Terry went out of her way to make this one special for me. My youngest son, his wife, and their two children came over and brought their grill. They then proceeded to grill steaks (and chicken for my wife). Add to that sliced tomatoes, baked potatoes, broccoli casserole, and you had a meal fit for a king.

My wife also made a special dessert composed of cherries, some kind of cream filler, and graham crackers. It is wonderful. I ate and ate and ate and I was stuffed. Then they all presented me with a new XM radio for my car. My wife has always had XM radio in her car, but I didn't have it in mine. I loved the gift and I was on a high.

Then my oldest son called. He and his family live in North Carolina. I miss them a lot and wished that they could have been here for the celebration. After I talked to them, I got in a really low, low state. So low that I decided to go to bed and it was only nine o'clock. I always get sleepy when I am the least bit depressed.

The next morning, two of our best friends called to say they wanted to go to our new church to hear my son preach. This really boosted me and I was on a high again. And they were very impressed with Sean's sermon. We went out to eat after the service and enjoyed each other's company for a couple of hours more. It was wonderful.

Then when I got home, I started thinking about all the people we left behind when we changed churches. We don't see that group of friends much any more and I miss them. I really do. It isn't that we don't ever see them, it is just that we don't see them like we used to. I got depressed again.

When Monday rolled around I was pretty much back to being myself. I am in my routine and Lord knows I love routine. Life is looking pretty good these days and I am enjoying each and every moment. Still sometimes the ways of the world lie heavy on my shoulders and I give in to self-pity or self-doubt. I think most of us do that from time to time.

I am not as bad about highs and lows as I used to be. In my younger days, I would soar with the good times and wallow in the bad.

My senior year in college I got upset about something (not being selected for "Who's Who") and stayed in my room for a week, missing classes and everything. I can't remember how I survived without food. I guess my roommate brought me stuff to feed my face. That sounds so ridiculous now, and also a little embarrassing. But that was me at that time in my life. When I got down I just wallowed in it.

These days I try to keep my emotions in control and go with the flow. Still sometimes, like this weekend, I become a human yo-yo. It doesn't happen often but it does still happen. I know it is tough on my family, but I would rather be mercurial than just the same old same old all the time. I don't know if my friends and family would agree with that. I don't think I better ask.

## *Magic Moments*

We all have magic moments in our lives. Those are the times that make us know life is worth living. They are also the times that lift our spirits and exalt our souls. Most of us do not get a lot of these moments but just when we think they are never going to come again one magically pops up.

The first magic moment I can remember must have happened when I was four or five years old. It was night time and we always had a family devotion before my brother and I went to bed. My mother had said the prayer that night because she had said, "Bless the poor, the sick, and the unfortunate," as she always did. I wanted to ask her if those three terms meant the same thing. In my young mind, if you were poor you were probably sick and therefore unfortunate.

My mother liked that I asked that question as she said it showed I was thinking. "You will always be a thinker," she said. Then she leaned down and whispered in my ear, "You are so special." There it was, my first magic moment. My mother, the most important person in my world, said I was special and I believed it.

The second magic moment came when I was thirteen. My mother had been sick for a few weeks and she was going to Greenville, South Carolina, for tests on a lymph node. We had all gathered to pray about this.

About a week or more after she had been to Greenville, I came home from school to find my mother delirious with joy. "It's benign," she said, and I had magic moment number two. I became just as delirious as she was. I was on top of the world.

Of course the magic from this moment didn't last. A few months later when she was still having trouble, they tested her again and this time it came back as cancer. Magic moments are what they say they are—moments. You have to grab on to them while you can and not expect them to last forever.

It took a while for any more magic moments to come into my life. The next one came about fifteen years later and it happened when I heard the word "yes" from the woman I had asked to be my wife. I was in my late twenties at the time and really thought I would never find the person I wanted to marry. I was picky, picky, picky.

When I did find The One, I panicked that maybe she would not want me. So when I finally did get up the nerve to ask her to marry me I really didn't know if she would say yes. But she did. She said yes and that was the most magical of moments. I have only proposed once in my life and I have only been accepted once, and having that kind of love for a lifetime makes my life a total magical moment.

As life goes on, magic moments keep coming. The first time I heard the words "I think we are going to have a baby," I was scared to death and thrilled to the moon. And years later when I heard the words "It's a girl" and I knew I finally had a granddaughter, my heart almost stopped.

The great thing about it all is that as long as you live the potential for magic moments can continue. The secret is in knowing when they happen and appreciating them as long as you can.

## *Is That a Backlash I Hear?*

Have you been to the movies lately? I have, but then it is my business to go to the movies since I'm a film critic. This means that I see just about everything Hollywood puts out there and let me tell you it is getting tougher and tougher to stomach some of what they are presenting.

Every time I see a Judd Apatow movie I wonder where this man's head is. It seems he has an entirely alien concept of what is funny. He seems to think if you string together enough profanity and sexual four letter words then you have a comedy. Then a movie like *Forgetting Sarah Marshall* comes along and you have to endure male nudity in the first scene.

Will Ferrell thought this movie was so funny that he added some male nudity of his own to the film *Step Brothers*. In neither case was it funny. And most of the people I saw in the theaters looked embarrassed rather than entertained.

Now along comes the movie *Fireproof*. It opened on only eight hundred screens as compared to the thousands of screens big movies open on. But it was the number three grossing film in the country on opening day. Its per screen average propelled it to this lofty rank. And you could just see the "suits" in Hollywood scratching their heads and asking, "Wha…?"

*Fireproof* is a movie about morals and values and it is drawing big crowds. The only star in the film is Kirk Cameron, but it's the story that's drawing people in. People are desperate for a film that doesn't embarrass them and actually has a moral to it.

A few nights ago, my wife and I went to a new restaurant in Warner Robins, Georgia. As we entered the door we noticed there was a passage of scripture painted above it. While we were there, the chef, who is the woman for whom the restaurant is named, came out and talked with us. She shared her life story with us and it was one of faith and commitment.

The restaurant seems to be doing a booming business and I attribute some of its success to the moral character of this lady. She sets the tone for the restaurant and people have responded. Now the food is also good and without that I don't think the restaurant would thrive. But this combination of good food and morality is a winner.

I realize I could be coming off as a religious zealot, but let me press on. I watched the *Saddleback* forum that Rick Warren hosted. Never in my lifetime have I heard the two presidential candidates discus their faith like McCain and Obama did in that setting. Of course there were rumblings in the media that it never should have happened, but I'm thankful it did.

I think Americans are getting sick of the lack of morals we are faced with every day, particularly in entertainment. We are also seeking some return to the old days when morals mattered. Is it some organized movement? No. It's just a flame of discontent that has sprung up as people have finally gotten fed up with all the immorality around them.

Now the success of *Fireproof* is not going to change the face of Hollywood overnight, but it might just make the big studio bosses do some reevaluating. And a few restaurants having moral leadership are not a beacon to a new world, but it might be a glimmer.

Something has to change in our world and I hope there is a backlash against the smut we have seen filling our lives. You can stand up against it with your entertainment dollars. Money, or lack of it, always hits them where it hurts.

## *What Happened to the Sting?*

For most of my life I have had a fear of dentists. I associate visits to their offices with pain, pain, and more pain. And besides the pain there is that awful whirring of the gadgets and gizmos as they drill into your teeth. The sounds alone are enough to make me want to head for the door.

I'm sure my family started me going to a dentist at an early age, but the first visit I remember was going to Dr. Salters for a filling. I kept saying I didn't need to go until the pain outweighed my fear. Then I reluctantly agreed I might need to have something done.

Once at the office, I began to get that clammy awful feeling you get when you know something horrible is headed your way. I felt like that little bib they put on me was going to choke me and that suction thing they put in my mouth was going to pull my brains out. Then they brought out the needle—the big needle! It looked about a foot long. Then the dreaded words were said, "This is going to sting a little."

Little, hah! It felt like that needle was going through my mouth and was going to come out through my jaw. I tried to holler for him to stop but I was afraid the needle would go through my tongue. Somehow I survived and then my whole face went numb. It wasn't just the area around my tooth, my whole face went numb!!

I closed my eyes and tried to relax and think of something—anything else. That's when the sound of the drill bored into my brain. I could hear it and I could feel it even though the numbness was complete. It was that grinding and vibrating that was just the worst feeling ever.

Somehow I survived, but in truth I have avoided dentists for most of my adult life. I have gone only when I have had to go. I haven't done regular checkups, just visits when I needed something done.

Anyway, a few weeks ago I decided I would have my teeth cleaned. While I was there, the dentist said I had a spot underneath one of my crowns that needed a filling. He said they could take care of it that day. Immediately all my dentist horror stories came into my mind.

The dental assistant came in and swabbed something on to my gum. Shortly thereafter the dentist came in and began to massage the gum. As he did he put the needle in my mouth. I kept waiting for the sting of pain and it never came. Honestly, I never felt a thing. What has happened? How can they give a shot and it not cause pain?

Then when they started drilling the sound and vibrations weren't even bad. I stayed calm and composed while they got my tooth back to where it should be. It was a non-bad experience. Well, I was going to say pleasant but that would be taking things a little too far.

I walked out of the dentist's office feeling like a new man. Things have really improved in the dental field. Just about everything is better. But there are still two things that are not. One, I didn't get a sucker. And two, the price has gotten worse. You still get stung but in a different way.

## *Nobody's Perfect*

Why is it that we strive so hard for perfection? We know there is never going to be any human being on earth who achieves that goal, but yet we keep pushing and struggling to get to ultimate perfection. Is it something we're taught or is it something innately in us that makes us want to be perfect?

We know that if we analyze something enough we can find some fault with it, but yet we rate or score events or people on a rate of 1 to 10—with 10 being perfect. We do this with everything from *Dancing with the Stars* to the Olympics. Plus who can ever forget the movie *10* when Bo Derek was judged to be a perfect 10.

I discussed this need for perfection with my friend, writer Augusta Trobaugh. I made mention of something being perfect and she said something like didn't we wish it was.

She then stated or quoted something about man being born with a need to strive for perfection. In other words we can't help it. We are destined to always want things to be better and that's what keeps us going in many instances.

I do think we get close to perfection at various times in our lives. I remember when I was nine or ten years old. I was in a field near our house flying a kite. It was in March, I think, and the sun was unusually warm for that month. The wind was blowing and the kite was soaring. I was feeling good and couldn't think of a worry in the world that I had. I made a mental note to myself to always remember this "perfect" time.

Strangely this day has stuck with me all these years. It was a day I was carefree and I knew it and appreciated it. That's important. We should recognize those near-perfect times in our lives and mark them down. Then we can pull them out and use them to balance the times that aren't so good.

Life is a balance of good times and bad times. Hopefully, the good days outnumber the bad days. If they do, well, we are lucky. We are never going to be perfect and times are never going to be perfect but, oh, the times when we get close are the times that make living worthwhile.

There is something inside us that makes us want perfection. It is a yearning that we can't explain. It is that need to have heaven on earth. It can frustrate us, and can make us weary; but for most of us the race is always on. We need to get better. We do get better. We enjoy life more when we are better. The secret is in the search.

Nobody is perfect, but the striving to be so is the pleasure. Just to know that heaven is within our grasp provides us with the joy of living.

## *The Memory Keeper*

Since my latest book is titled *The Sunrise Remembers* (Mercer University Press) I have been focusing on "memories" as I have been out and about publicizing the book. I have talked to school groups, social clubs, libraries, etc., about the need to collect the memories we have of our families.

What I have heard over and over is that most families have a "memory keeper" who knows all the stories—the legends and the lore. It is usually Uncle Bill or Aunt Mary and they are the ones who can visit and tell one story after another about the family. But the big question is whether this "memory keeper" has committed these stories to paper (or computer).

We are not a nation that talks much to each other anymore. It used to be that families would sit down at the supper table and just talk about their day or about something happening within the family. Now with TV, computers, and two wage earners with job responsibilities, we don't have the time to set aside a "talking" period. So any story time we might have had in the past is now gone.

So how do we keep our stories from being lost? Easy, we become a country of journalers. I encourage people from the earliest ages to be journalers, to write down the stories of the families or to recall important events that have occurred. If you do it every day it becomes habit-forming and not a burden. It also becomes fun.

Then at some point you gather these thoughts and descriptions into some kind of book or notebook and have it passed along to the next generation. And as each generation adds their stories you get a multigenerational document that holds the history.

After I gave a talk on this subject recently, a lady came up to speak to me. She had decided during my talk to tell each member of her family to bring a story about their grandfather when they came for

Christmas. She is going to collect them and keep them safe. Then next Christmas she is going to pick another relative and ask for stories about them. This is going to go on for many Christmases to come and the outcome will be a description of the family members that can be handed down. I think this is a wonderful idea.

We never know how important our memories are to us. I asked a class of fourth graders to tell me their earliest memory. One little boy said he fell off his bike and busted his knee when he was four. A little girl told me she lost her favorite stuffed bunny when she was three. And on and on they went.

Finally a little girl raised her hand and told me she remembered her parents getting a divorce. Then she added "and I wasn't even born yet." I was stunned but then realized this event had made such an imprint on her mind all her life that she thought she remembered it. Memories are made from such impressive moments.

I have written five books and they all come from my journals. I didn't plan it that way but that's what happened. Still even if I hadn't collected my stories into book form they still would have been important. They are the history of my life and that of the Coopers and the Kershaws. I have those stories to hand down to my sons and to their children.

Find the memory keeper in your family or become that person yourself. The rewards of being that person are huge—and they last for more than a lifetime.

## *The Georgia and Jackie Show*

A hundred years ago when I was in high school, one of my classmates and I decided we wanted to have a radio show. Her name is Georgia Young and she was as impetuous as I was, plus she was the Judy Garland to my Mickey Rooney. It was basically, "Let's put on a show in the barn," and off we went.

We contacted the people at the local radio station, WPCC, and, lo and behold, they said yes! So started *The Georgia and Jackie Show*. We played requests and related school news every afternoon Monday through Friday for a half hour each afternoon. Did we feel like big time celebrities? You betcha.

Of course, the glory can only last so long and then something like this becomes work. Too much work for me, so I decided to bow out leaving Georgia to fend for herself. And she didn't miss a beat. She became *The Georgia Show* and expanded it to an hour each day.

I tell you this because this morning I was on the phone to WPCC in Clinton where they were celebrating the fiftieth anniversary of the station. Georgia, who lives in Clinton, was there live and I was an invited "guest" on the phone. It was loads of fun and a good trip down memory lane for the listeners. We even played a couple of songs from our era.

In order to prepare for this morning, Georgia and I had had a two-hour conversation a few nights ago. I asked about different people from our graduating class. Georgia knew every one and has kept up with most of them. She is amazing.

I found myself asking about couples who I knew were married, and then adding "Are they still together?" Sadly many of them are not, but the majority are. I also found myself asking about some people I didn't know too well, "Are they still alive?" A good many of them aren't.

As Georgia and I talked, I found myself falling back into the life we had in those days of high school. Names came to me that I had not thought about in decades. My class only had about ninety members, maybe less, so knowing most of the class was not a problem. A large number of my classmates have stayed in the Clinton area.

In April of next year, we are having a class reunion. It will be the first reunion I attend since my father and stepmother died. In that respect, it will be the most stress-free visit I will have had in many, many years. I look forward to being back and seeing the friends from my childhood.

I do miss the Clinton of my early years. It was a town that provided its citizens with security and happiness. Clintonians looked after each other. If you had an illness or were going through hard times a helping hand was always available. I know when my mother was sick with cancer the kindness of our friends and even strangers was amazing.

It was good to be back in Clinton this morning even if it was by phone. "The Georgia and Jackie Show" was not long lived but it is a bright memory for me. There have been a lot of TV and radio shows since then but that show on WPCC influenced them all.

## *Guilt by Association*

Remember when you were a kid how your parents were always harping on who you chose as friends. I know mine did. My mother would tell me over and over that you are judged by the company you keep. There were definitely people I liked that she didn't, and she would tell me over and over to stay away from them. Sometimes I listened and sometimes I didn't.

It is true we are influenced by our peers, and the crowd with which we choose to run. How much they influence us varies from situation to situation. Some barely have any impact and others influence us a lot.

In this last presidential election a lot of fuss was made over who influenced the candidates. One of the big arguments was that sixties radical reformer William Ayers was a major influence on the life and philosophies of Barack Obama. This argument wasn't decisive in the election, but it did get some traction.

I never gave much thought to this argument one way or the other *until* I got an e-mail from a friend of mine. Attached to it was an article she had written about William Ayers. Again I wasn't too interested until I saw a line that asked if Jackie K. Cooper was guilty of being a radical because he had been on a panel with Mr. Ayers.

Honestly, I had forgotten all about it. It occurred when I was invited to the South Carolina Book Festival a few years ago. I was asked to participate in a panel discussion of memoirs. I remember Dori Sanders was also on the panel but I had forgotten the other two members—until I read that article.

Yes, William Ayers was on that panel. He had written a book about his life. I remember him now and how abrasive he was. He seemed to have a chip on his shoulder a mile high. He also did not mingle well with others. He stayed apart from the rest of us and never asked any information about us in a generally friendly way.

Still, I was on a panel with Bill Ayers and in some people's minds that would brand me with the same brush people would apply to him. It doesn't matter that we are poles apart philosophically and politically. The fact we shared a close proximity on the stage would be enough.

Is that fair? I don't think so. I also didn't think it was totally fair when the accusations were made against Obama, although he did have a closer relationship with the man than I had. Still that guilt thing attaches regardless of the circumstances.

So here I am with William Ayers in my past, and I didn't even remember it. With that old Kevin Bacon six-degrees-of-separation thing I guess we are all linked to the good and the bad throughout the world. So we better not cast aspersions too hastily on people about their past associations. The next one getting some mud flung on them just might be you.

## *Is Honesty the Best Policy?*

Last weekend I taught a course at Kennesaw College for the Georgia Writers Association. It was an hour and a half on "Being a Critic—for Fun, Fame and Profit?" You notice the question mark at the end of the title. That refers to the profit aspect.

I went through the whole history of how I, Jackie K. Cooper from Clinton, South Carolina, became a film and book critic. It was a long journey full of wonderful coincidences and amazing mentors.

At the end of the session, I was talking about what goes into a book review. I stated I always try to find something good in even the worst book and something not so perfect to add to a rave review. I always try to remind people this is just one man's opinion and not anything more.

Having said this I added I always try to send the author a copy of my review. I usually Google them and find a website which will have a "Contact Me" area. I then send the author an e-mail which states, "My review of (the book) has been posted to my website www.jackiekcooper.com. This review also appeared in my newspapers."

I have been doing this for ages and frequently get a note back from the author thanking me for the review. From these correspondences, I have struck up a friendship with various authors. But friendship or not I still give an honest review of the books I select. This sometimes makes it a little awkward, but I don't think I have lost any friends over my reviews.

Recently I did have one friend tell me if I did not like his book just not to review it (or at least not have the review published). Still I think most writers agree with my attitude as a writer which is that any publicity is good publicity.

*Jackie K. Cooper*

When I attended the Dahlonega Book Festival this year, I was sitting with some authors and mentioned to them an incident that had happened with my book reviews. I had sent a notice of my review of a book to an author. It was a mixed review. I had found some things I liked and some I didn't. Well, shortly after I sent the notice to the author he responded with an angry message about it. He said if I sent him notice of a review that he should reasonably expect it to be a "good" review. He hardly expected it to be unfavorable, and that I was never to review any more of his books.

Of course, I can review any book I choose to review, but I probably will make a note to leave this author's books off my desk. I thought his response was extremely thin skinned and touchy. But the authors who I told this story to had mixed feelings.

One agreed totally with me and said he had used my reviews to help improve his writing. Another said I should never send notice of a review unless it was a good review. She said that even mildly negative reviews can be terribly hurtful.

I don't know if I am going to change my policy or not. I certainly don't want to cause anyone grief by what I write, but if I'm not honest in my opinion of what use is it? I am lucky enough to have newspapers and other media like my reviews enough to pay for them. That makes me a professional critic per se. It doesn't however mean that my opinion is any more credible than that of someone else.

## *Love What's There*

Once upon a time I lived in Clinton, South Carolina. My family lived on Holland Street and we were a typical group: father, mother, and two children. We weren't rich but we weren't poor either. My brother and I had two parents we loved and who loved us. Neither of my parents drank and they were loving rather than abusive. I thought everyone's home was like that. Then I met Chuck.

Chuck's grandmother lived across the street from my house. He would come and visit her and somehow the two of us met and got to know each other. We were in the same grade at school but really hadn't been aware of each other until we met at his grandmother's house. But friendships form fast in the South and we became the very best of friends.

It was a few months after that meeting that I met Chuck's father. Chuck and I were standing outside the drug store uptown where my mother was getting some things. A man lurched by, obviously intoxicated, and stumbled on down the street. Chuck turned to me and said, "That's my dad."

I don't remember how I responded, but I know I was shocked. I was even more shocked when I met Chuck's mother and smelled alcohol on her breath. Both of Chuck's parents were alcoholics and made his life miserable. He rarely had the right food to eat. His clothes were always too small for him. If it hadn't been for his grandmother I don't know how he would have survived.

At this time, rehab was not a common thing and people with alcohol problems rarely got help. They were known as the town drunks and as such were tolerated. Eventually they usually drank themselves to death.

One time after Chuck had found his dad drunk on the street and helped him home, I asked him why he bothered. He looked at me and said simply, "I love him." By this time I had had it with both his parents and I came back with. "How could you? They both treat you bad all the time."

Then he answered, "I love the good in them."

A few weeks ago, I was watching a television program. In it a private detective was hired to find a woman's missing teenage daughter. At the end of the show he found the runaway girl and reunited her with her mother. But as she talked with the daughter the mother became frustrated and told the detective, "I don't even know who she is."

"Love what's there," he stated.

"But she has hurt me and done things I don't understand," the mother protested.

"Love what's there," the detective repeated.

"Why does she do this?" the mother asked. "Why does she do the things she does? She is ruining my life and hers."

And the detective answered for the third time, "Love what's there."

Finally the mother understood and embraced her daughter. The girl, though rigid at first, relaxed and hugged her back.

None of us are perfect. The longer I live the more I understand that fact all too well. All of us need for someone to love the good in us, and we in turn need to love the good in those around us. We may not understand why people do what they do but in the end we simply have to love what's there.

## *A Very Thankful Day*

This is one of those times when I just try to steer clear of the news. Usually I am a news fanatic. During the past election I was glued to the TV set and loved hearing all the "talking heads" ramble on and on. But lately the economic news has been so bad that I have just tried to shut my eyes and ears and ride it out by being oblivious to it.

It's not working. Somehow the information about the problems of banks, carmakers, credit card companies, and a host of others have seeped into my brain. I don't want to hear about it and yet I do. I spout that ignorance is bliss, but in my heart I know that's stupid.

It is easy to slip into depression about it all. There doesn't seem to be an upside, yet I know there has to be. This is where your faith comes into play. Just believing that someone is in control of all this is comforting.

That's why on Thanksgiving I will say a special prayer of thanks for many, many things. At the top of my list is my faith. If I didn't have it I would have nothing. And I am so thankful my family and I share the same faith. It is awkward having your son be your pastor, but it is also a very comforting thing knowing that we can worship in a church where he is the leader.

My family is next. My youngest son, his wife, and children moved back to Perry this year. Having them in the same town where we get to see them every day is wonderful. I always wanted my grandchildren to be so familiar with my house that they were comfortable in it and I think that's true of Genna and Walker.

I am also so grateful we are all healthy. You hear of so many people suffering from such awful health problems, so if you and your family are healthy you are truly blessed. I also try never to take my health for granted. You have to work on staying healthy.

Next is my gratitude for my friends. This was the year that we changed churches and it was a major incident in our lives. Most of our friends were/are friends from that church and to leave was traumatic to say the least. Still we don't regret moving to the church where our son is preaching.

Our friends have been wonderful about keeping in touch. We don't see them as often as we would like, but we know they are still there for us as we are for them. Friends are the seasoning of our lives. They add the additional flavor and make life richer.

As I said, there are some tough times ahead for us. This economy thing is scary but even in the tough times we do have things to be thankful for, such as faith, family, friends, and health.

This Thanksgiving may be just the time for us to count our blessings and to give thanks. It also might be the time to be vigilant as to how you can help somebody else. There are people in need, and we need to help them.

## *Season of Hope*

Well, December has arrived and we have now entered into what I like to call "the season of hope." The days leading up to Christmas have always seemed that way to me. It is a time of hope, a time of anticipation, a time of miracles. Maybe it was all those old movies that made me think hope, anticipation and miracles could occur. Hollywood sold it and I bought it.

Recently I have heard a lot of people talking about hope. Maybe it is because the economy is in such a downturn, or that people are losing their jobs. People say things like, "I hope things get better" or "I hope I don't lose my job." They hope, I hope, we all hope.

A couple was telling me about their own experience with hope. It seems when they got married they just naturally assumed they would have many children. Not just one or two—they wanted a lot. But as the days, months and years passed nothing happened. They were stunned.

They went to doctor after doctor and did all the things the medical profession told them to do. Still no child. When the husband's brother and his new wife found they were pregnant after only a few months of marriage, this couple hit rock bottom. Depression was rampant and hope was nowhere to be found.

The woman told me she finally decided she was through trying to make it happen. She had thought by force of will she could make them have a baby. She admitted to herself she couldn't do it and just turned it over to God. Her husband said he did the same thing. When they placed their hope and trust in God, they got pregnant.

After eight years, they finally were going to have a baby. And that baby was followed by another baby, who was followed by another baby, who was followed by another baby. They ended up with four wonderful children. In a helpless situation, they found hope and hope led to happiness.

Another woman told me that in 2001 she was diagnosed with breast cancer. By the time they discovered it, it had already metastasized. She was given a fifty-fifty chance of surviving. She said she just knew this was it, and that she had been given a death sentence that couldn't be changed. She felt hopeless.

During the next days and weeks, she moved in a fog, deep in depression and full of anger. Then one day she found the faith of her childhood and told God she wanted to be his child in any way he wanted. If He wanted her to continue living that was fine and if He wanted her to come to Heaven that was fine too. She was full of hope as to what would be the outcome, because either way she couldn't lose.

The lady told me she was "born" on that day that she made that decision. That was in 2001. "I am now eight years old," she told me with a beaming smile. And she is full of hope for the future.

Do things always work out this way? No. But there is always hope that they will. That's what makes this season of hope so special. December is the month of miracles and it heralds the season of hope.

## *Car Faith*

When I buy a car I keep it for a long, long time. The one I have now is a Saturn and it has 234,000 miles on it. It is six years old. Usually when we buy a new car I give Terry the old one and I take the new one. At least that's what we did when I was still working in Macon and had a sixty mile commute every day. But when we bought a new car last year Terry got it and I kept the old car.

This car and I have a bond. There is just something about it that makes me feel safe. I haven't named it or done anything crazy like that, though I know people who do. I just call it "car" when the mood comes over me to have a conversation with, well, my car.

In this car, the service engine light has been on for years. My mechanic told me that if it still ran good to ignore that light warning. And so I have. It is there and I just ignore it and drive on. It has worked out fine.

A few days ago, I was on my way to Macon. I was introducing the speaker for the Sidney Lanier Cottage Autumn Array of Authors. I had been on the interstate for about five miles when the service light came on—the one with the wrench icon. At the same time, the motor shut down and the car began to coast to a stop. Another light came on saying "car slowing down" or something inane like that.

I pulled off the road and brought the car to a complete stop. This is when I began talking to the car with devotion and desperation. "Please start back up!" I begged. Then I added how much I loved the car and how good it had been to me. "Just a little more," I urged.

I turned the switch and the motor came to life—with the "service" and wrench icon still showing. I decided I should drive the car fairly slowly so as not to aggravate the situation. I set the cruise control on fifty and proceeded to Macon.

The car got me there even if that blasted light did stay on the entire time. I got there with five minutes to spare, which was plenty of time for me to get ready to introduce Man Martin, the guest author for that night.

When the program was over I rushed to my car hoping it would get me home safely, one more time. Once again I had a conversation with the car where I enumerated its good points. I turned the switch and the motor came to life, and, believe it or not, the service light and wrench icon were not to be seen.

Coming home I kept the cruise control on fifty again. I called my wife and alerted her I might have some trouble and if I wasn't home in fifty minutes to come looking for me (by the way I had one bar of battery left on my cell phone so I couldn't count on being able to make another call.).

When I got home, I breathed a sigh of relief and gently patted the hood of the car. It had done its job. You know it struggled to cover those miles. Other cars might not have made it but my car did. All it took was a little faith. Now if I can only coax it into running for another two hundred thousand miles. Hey, it could happen!

## *Quiet Desperation*

In these days of economic unrest I find myself thinking more and more about people who live lives of quiet desperation. These are people who are just hanging on, waiting for the other shoe to drop. It might be a cut in pay, a job loss, an illness, the end of a relationship, or something else horrible, but some people need only one more nudge to push them over the edge.

One of my friends told me the other day that he almost gets physically sick each morning when he wakes up thinking about having to go to his job. He hates it that much. But he has no other opportunity and he needs a paycheck. He is going to have to be at this job for at least another ten years, if he lasts that long.

Another friend of mine hates his job, too, but he has to have health insurance. So he is stuck with a barely-get-through-the-day situation that will go on for years. He is grateful to have the job, but he just doesn't like what he's doing. He says every eight-hour day is more like eighteen hours.

Then there is my friend who is a film critic. For twenty years she worked for a large newspaper and built up a name for herself. She also earned a good salary. Then came this recession and the cutbacks began. She was the first to go. Who needs movie reviews in this downbeat world?

Now she has no retirement and no prospects of employment unless she wants to start all over in another field. It seems that when the cutbacks start the entertainment writers and then the feature writers are the first thrown overboard. Luckily my friend saved some of her earnings over the years but that won't last forever.

Then there are the folks who thought they were okay with their job and then a major illness came their way. Sickness takes everything else off the board. It is the big trump card that changes the rules of the game.

Last Sunday night my son came up to me and said, "You won't believe what happened!" When he told me, it wasn't as bad as I had feared. He had backed his car into a tree and had ruined the bumper. This happened to be the new car he had just bought his wife and I could tell that was his big worry.

I asked what she had said and he said, "She reminded me of what you always say: if money can fix it, it isn't a problem." That's my philosophy, and that's why I respect illness as the game changer. Money can not buy you health in many instances.

Anyway, there's a lot of bad news going around this holiday season. To get by people are going to need the three *F*s: faith, family, and friends. I believe those are the only things that can get you through. So give a thought to being supportive of someone this year. I don't mean in a monetary way, though that might be nice if you have it. I mean, be a friend, offer an encouraging word, share a meal or even a prayer. We are all in this together and nobody gets out alive, so during our time on earth we need to help alleviate the "quiet desperation" others are feeling.

## *Yes, Santa Claus, There Is a Virginia*

Dear Santa Claus,

    I hear you are having a rough time of it lately. You don't feel enough people believe in you and are actually thinking of chucking the whole Christmas Eve toy ride around the world. You stated you think people would rather believe in ogres and talking donkeys than believe in you. Not so, Mr. C., not so!

    Years ago a little girl named Virginia asked if you were real and a newspaper editor answered her question with a resounding *yes*! Now I would like to tell you about another little girl named Virginia. She was born Virginia Kershaw in Gadsden, Alabama. She was the youngest girl in a family of eight children and she grew up loving Christmas and you.

    When she became an adult, she got married and moved to Clinton, South Carolina. There she and her husband Tom raised their two sons Tommy and Jackie. Virginia loved her family and she loved Christmas. She loved the tree, the carols, the presents, and the joy of it all. She also knew what the true meaning of the celebration was and she passed that all along to her sons.

    Each year she tried to outdo the last Christmas in decorations and ingenious gifts, but she also made sure the very best gifts were the ones that came from you. She liked the wide-eyed wonderment that appeared in her boys' eyes when she told them how you made all the toys at the North Pole and then delivered them all around the world on Christmas Eve night.

    Sadly one year she got sick on Christmas Day and soon she was gone. Still her spirit and enthusiasm kept Christmas alive for her family. It was a day she was always mentioned and always remembered. It became known as "the day Mother loved best."

Over the years, the boys let their enthusiasm for Christmas slip but once they too were married the magic and the spirit came back. They may not have done it as enthusiastically as she had, but they always did their best for Mother. Their children had learned about you and your special job at Christmas.

So, Mr. Claus, don't give up on us yet. I know there are still many, many believers out there. I see it in the face of my granddaughter Genna, my mother's namesake. The enthusiasm she has for you and this day are part of her heritage. Her blue eyes (just like her great-grandmother's) light up when you mention that Christmas is almost here. She gets that second burst of energy and makes sure that we all know Santa is coming.

There are too many things in this world that are being swept away by the passage of time. You, Mr. Claus, do not need to be one of them. You are the epitome of hope and happiness for some. If you can miraculously circle the globe delivering presents then maybe other miraculous things can occur.

Knowing you and loving you does not mean that children can't get the religious aspects of the season. After all having a baby be born to save the world is about as miraculous as it gets.

So pick yourself up, dust yourself off, and get going. This is no time to get yourself into a snit. Children are still children and all children need Santa. And the child inside all of us does too.

See you soon!<br>
Your friend and believer,<br>
Jackie Kershaw Cooper

## *The Ballad of Bambo*

It was a good Christmas this year. My oldest son who lives in Durham came down with his wife and one-year-old daughter. My wife and I drove down to St. Pete and picked up my mother-in-law and brought her back to our house. My youngest son and his family already live in Perry so they were in and out of the house sharing the joys of the season.

It was a good Christmas this year except.... The exception was that on the night after Christmas my wife, mother-in-law, oldest son, his wife and daughter, and I went to Warner Robins to eat at an Italian restaurant. We took two cars since there were too many of us to fit in my son's car.

On the way back we were almost to the turnoff to our subdivision when a deer ran out on to the street and into our car. I managed to swerve so that he went down the right side of the car instead of straight into it. Still the right front fender and the right side passenger doors were damaged.

When last seen, the deer was walking back towards the side of the road. When we got home, we called the police and told them to be on the lookout for a groggy deer, then I called my insurance company. The good thing is that none of us were hurt; the bad thing is the inconvenience of having to have the car fixed.

The next day I was telling my grandchildren about it and Genna asked if it was a baby deer or a big deer. I assured her it was a big mean deer. Then she asked if I killed it. I assured her I didn't and that the deer was back home in the woods. That's when my wife chimed in and said someone told her they saw it lying on the side of the road. So much for protecting my sensitive granddaughter.

When I got home I decided to create a story that would make Genna feel better. I titled the story "Bambo" and here it is.

Jackie K. Cooper

## Bambo

Once upon a time there was a little deer that lived in the forest. His name was Bambi, his mother had named him after her favorite movie. He lived with his mother and father as well as other forest creatures. They had a good life but as Bambi grew older he realized that the land of the machines was encroaching on their living area. This displeased him greatly. He always swore he would get revenge for being forced to live in a smaller and smaller area.

When he grew to adulthood he was elected leader of the forestry association. It was at this time his father decided he should not be called Bambi any longer. Because he was a fierce leader, his father said he should be called Bambo (He was a movie fan, too.). And Bambo he became.

Bambo lived a long life and took care of those who lived in the forest as best he could. But the land of machines continued to force them into smaller and smaller areas. It was totally frustrating to Bambo and he vowed one day he would make them pay.

When Bambo was reaching the end of his days, he decided the time was right. He made his plans carefully and staked out a place where he could watch the machines pass. One night he decided the time was right. He dug in his hooves and got ready to attack, and attack he did. He lunged at a sleek silver machine that was coming down the road.

As soon as he hit it Bambo knew he had done damage. At the same time, his heart just stopped and death came quickly, but not quickly enough to rob him of his satisfaction for striking a blow for the animals.

*The animals in the forest mourned the death of Bambo, but all agreed he had lived a wonderful life and more importantly had died an honorable death.*

## *Epilogue*

So on it goes, the journey continues through valleys and peaks. Life is a continuum that brings with it highs and lows. This traveler is getting a little more weary as the road continues. I have some new aches and pains that seem to inhabit my body; still what a delight it is to still be alert to the beauties of things that are offered.

Each day brings a new story, a new tale to tell. I find a renewal of my faith in my God, my family and my fellow man. Along the way I meet a few angels who whisper words of wisdom in my ears and make me realize what a jubilant experience life can be.

I hope you have enjoyed the stories I have provided for you this time and that you are anxious to hear more. As long as the mist parts and provides me with the memories of these tales gone by I will pass them on to you.

Until we meet again I wish you godspeed and God's blessings.

Jackie K. Cooper  
Perry, Georgia  
February 19, 2013